759.13q Wat   T 000914
Watson, Ernest W.
   Twenty painters and how they
work

Date Due			
1 Apr '60	31 Jan '61		
27 Apr '60	14 Feb '61		
14 May '60	6 Mar '61		
1 Jun '60	17 Apr '61		
28 Jun '60	9 May '61		
14 Jul '60	10 Jun '61		
29 Jul '60	14 Jul '61		
16 Sep '60	9 Aug '61		
1 Nov '60	30 Sep		
25 Nov '60	25 Oct '61		
20 Dec '60	11 Dec '61		
3 Jan '61	7-24-65		

TWENTY PAINTERS

TWENTY
PAINTERS

And how they work

by

ERNEST W. WATSON

WATSON-GUPTILL

PUBLICATIONS, INC.

New York

PREFACE

THESE chapters on twenty American painters were originally written as articles for AMERICAN ARTIST Magazine and were received with such enthusiasm that the publishers decided to bring them together in a book as a permanent record of the creative procedures of top American artists.

The interviews take the reader behind the scenes in the painters' studios and reveal much of the creative processes involved in their work. Some chapters are devoted largely to technical matters. They are discussions of the painter's materials—his colors, brushes, canvas, mediums—and demonstrations of how they are employed in the practice of his craft. They include notes on the uses of different kinds of varnishes, recipes for grounds and directions for underpainting and glazing. They contain much practical instruction on color and the techniques of brush and palette knife painting.

In some chapters the emphasis is on the purely creative—as distinct from the material—aspects of picturemaking. The development of the picture is sometimes demonstrated in sketches and step-by-step composition studies. Quotations of the painters' own words often contribute greatly to the understanding of their problems.

A few painters are studied largely from the biographical viewpoint because their background, their development as artists and the way in which they have organized their lives seemed to be the most useful contribution these particular men could make.

It will be seen that the purpose of this book, as of the articles when they first appeared in the magazine, is to offer instruction to students of contemporary art with its conflicting philosophies and its exciting experiments in new modes of expression. There are no non-objective or abstract painters among the twenty here assembled although in more than one the influence of the abstract school is clearly observed. By focusing upon representational painting it is believed that the aims of the author and the publishers coincide with the wishes of a very large art-loving and art-practicing public.

The contents of this book offer a variety of subject matter—nude figure, figure composition, portrait, still life, landscape and genre. It is hoped that in its pages the reader will find the inspiration and instruction to which he is entitled.

The publishers take this opportunity to express their gratitude to the artists for permission to print their stories in this book. They have been most cooperative in connection with the interviews, in supplying pictorial matter for the illustrations and in checking and approving all that has been written about them.

CONTENTS

COLOR PLATES

Louis Bosa

MYSELF 1950 OIL 14 x 8

Louis Bosa
an American painter who looks at life

"THE emotional experiences that the modern artist's work can arouse will be minor ones, unless he can seek, find, or help to create symbols ratified by society which can make his pictures in turn concrete symbols of dominant human interests."

These words, quoted from Lee Simonson's book, *Art Today,* come to mind as a fitting introduction to my comment on the work of Louis Bosa. For here is a painter who draws his inspiration directly from life and from nature, who is interested in humanity, not as cartoonist or as moralist with an ideological axe to grind, but rather as a fascinated observer of the comedy and tragedy of unchanging human nature. When he launches into essays like *Street Fight* and *Saturday Night* he does enter the realm of caricature, to be sure, but in many of his canvases his personages are only details of street scenes and landscapes. Yet they are much more than incidental spots of color, such as many painters introduce into their pictures merely for the sake of design. No matter how small in scale his people, they are the indispensable fulfillment of the over-all picture concept. Look at *Frank's Barber Shop,* for example; remove the gaunt pedestrian and you almost erase the painter's signature.

Thomas Craven, writing about Pieter Brueghel, said that this Flemish master "could not conceive of landscape except in human terms, and his renderings of it, broadly speaking, are harmonious adjustments of nature to the moods and activities of man." This quotation applies with equal fitness to the landscapes of Louis Bosa who, by the way, is a disciple of Brueghel.

Bosa is not much interested in painting landscapes—especially painting outdoors—except as a means of maintaining intimacy with nature. Nevertheless, he does considerable painting from nature to "brighten me up," as he says. He is in the habit of making weekend sorties from his Bucks County home for these brightening-up experiences. *Pheasant Hunters* is a good example of the pictures that come out of such sketching trips. (See color plate.)

The mood of Bosa's studio pictures is almost always sombre. His city subjects usually are found in drab streets of neglected areas peopled by the less prosperous of New York's millions. He has a rare genius for drawing out the spiritual essence of these dreary subjects. Rain, snow, and leaden skies conspire in many canvases to enhance the melancholy mood. Rural landscapes achieve the same end when painted in late evening or under night skies. Bosa's painted world is seldom bathed in sunlight.

His people likewise reflect the sombre mood. They are apprehensive; creeping stealthily along soggy streets, they cast furtive glances over their shoulders as though fearful of a surprise attack. They are never really merry, even when they go skating in Central Park or gather at the water's edge for a picnic. They are less like Brueghel's peasants, and are more suggestive of the types seen in the canvases of Hieronymus Bosch, who is also one of Bosa's graphic heroes.

But unlike Bosch, Bosa is not a moralist or satirist; there is in his work no trace of irony or sarcasm for the purpose of exposing and discrediting vice or folly. His

FISH STORY 1950 OIL 34 x 40

attitude toward the humble folk he portrays so well is one of sympathy and understanding, one might say *pity*, if that did not imply a looking-down-upon, which would be wholly out of character in the artist. But even in *Fish Story*—about as lighthearted a theme as Bosa paints—he has depicted the people of this sordid street with dramatic pathos. They are indeed a pitiable lot. His own self-portraits wear the same melancholy mask as do the frustrated inhabitants of his subject pictures.

The truth is that Bosa probably is not as preoccupied with the social aspects of his work as my comments might suggest. Bosa is first of all a painter. Like Rembrandt and Leonardo he follows people about in the streets because he is fascinated by the beauty of their ugliness. I have seen only one canvas which suggests a satirical motive—the picture called *Carnegie Hall,* a close-up of one of the boxes in that famous auditorium. But the picture is not successful. Instead of caricatures of dowagers and their bored escorts, he gives us fishwives dressed up in the habiliments of high society.

It should be evident that Bosa does not rely upon professional models to any extent. His types are people he sees and sketches in neighborhood bars and restaurants. He spends hours wandering about with his sketchbook. If he brings home something he plans to use in a picture, he begins work on it at once while impressions are fresh. He goes back to the subject for further study again and again. He will fake nothing. The store fronts in *Fish Story* were copied literally from some seen on old buildings on the west side of

New York. *Frank's Barber Shop* is almost a portrait of a desolate establishment in the same part of town.

Bosa doesn't sit in his studio coaxing imagination. His canvases always begin with something seen in real life, but the episode may be little more than the seed of an idea that germinates and develops in the artist's creative mind.

Bosa's technical procedure is simple. Most of his early pictures were painted in the traditional, direct method, but he has become interested in underpainting and glazing. His palette is quite restricted, and he does all his work with three bristle brushes of varying sizes and one small sable with which he paints figures and small details. He has a preference for long and narrow canvases, both vertical and horizontal.

Bosa, though of a buoyant, happy disposition, and a great fun-maker, is temperamental in his work. He will paint only when the spirit moves. That is never in the morning; he prefers the mellow atmosphere of evening, and enjoys listening to good music while working.

Like so many painters, Bosa devotes some of his time to teaching. He has taught at the Art Students League of New York in winter, and in Rockport in the summer. He is called upon often to serve on juries for national exhibitions. In 1944, Bosa was awarded the Altman Prize of the National Academy of Design, only to have the decision withdrawn because, although a citizen, he is not American-born. In 1944, also, he won the $1,500 third prize in the Portrait of America Competition. His painting was reproduced on the 1945 Pepsi-Cola Portrait of America Calendar.

FRANK'S BARBER SHOP   1945   OIL ON PANEL   12 x 16

Other awards accorded him include a $500 prize in each of Pepsi-Cola's 1946 and 1947 exhibitions, a $100 first prize in 1946 at the Rockport Art Association, a $1,000 award from the Academy of Arts and Letters in 1948, a $700 first prize at the Los Angeles Fair that same year, and in 1949 a $900 Purchase Prize at the University of Illinois' all-American Exhibition, as well as the Audubon Artists' Gold Medal.

At this writing, he has held four one-man shows in New York and is represented in many collections, public and private, such as those of the Philadelphia Museum of Art, the Worcester and Springfield (Massachusetts) museums, the Montclair Art Museum, Clearwater Museum, Wilmington Art Center, the Encyclopaedia Britannica, and International Business Machines.

Louis Bosa was born in 1905 in Codroipo, Italy. "For years," says Bosa, "Codroipo was a town of tailless cats, as a result of a mania that took possession of me at the age of nine. I stroked the cat until it was asleep, then chopped off its tail, and in the basement hung a line of cat tails, each neatly labeled with the name of the cat's owner. When I was seen on the street, the possessor of a pet cat would call excitedly, 'Hide the cat! Here comes Gigi Bosa!'"

Bosa urges us not to judge him too harshly for this youthful perversion. "Today," he says, "I wouldn't hurt a fly and, after all, do not very respectable people trim dogs' ears and dock horses' tails for no more praiseworthy reasons?"

In spite of this moral lapse, Louis' interest in animals was not wholly sadistic. "Even now," he says, "I have to

BY THE EAST RIVER   1950   OIL   34 x 24

restrain myself around any animal, especially a funny looking one, because I'm apt to become fond of it and my collection of pets can rapidly get out of hand. The ground floor of my summer studio has housed a menagerie of pigs, chickens, and ducks at various times. When I was a child, the cellar of our house contained cats, birds, and even trained rats which I harnessed to little coaches. Feeding this collection of animals made such inroads on my father's store of salami and cheese that he finally lost patience, put the entire zoo in a bag and dropped it in the river. My heart was broken and I determined to drown myself, but my attempt was a failure and I came home late at night, dripping wet and miserable."

Bosa has a country home and studio in Bucks County, Pennsylvania. The house is an old log cabin which was in an advanced state of decay when the Bosas bought it. They have restored it and made it an idyllic retreat where they spend much time in the warmer months. Louis is an excellent craftsman both in wood and in metal, and all of the labor of restoration was his own. He went to great pains in giving all new construction the semblance of age. His front door is made of three wide planks which he antiqued in an original manner. He took them out into a field, piled a quantity of hay on them, poured kerosene over all, lighted a match and walked away. When, some time later, he remembered them, he found them in a too-antiqued condition and had to remove some of "time's" ravages, with plane and steel brush.

Bosa, like most artists, has experimented with various painting philosophies. For a time he was interested in impressionism, chose Renoir as his model. He finally discovered Bosa, and has established himself as an original painter with a highly individual response to his environment. He is not likely to be tempted by the ivory tower philosophy so popular in those avant-garde establishments on Fifty-seventh Street which insist that only the vistas seen by inward looking are worthy subjects for the painter's eyes. That is a soft haven for both sterility and conceit. Bosa is too much engrossed by the human drama to dally with esoteric trifles. Without calling him a Brueghel, a Goya, or a Daumier, we can say that his art springs from the same kind of passion for interpretation of contemporary life as was basic in the genius of those masters.

Thus far, Bosa has not been influenced by the old world decadence which has turned some of America's good talent into paths of frustration. By following the dictates of his own warm interest in the contemporary human drama, he has developed a highly individual philosophy and a language which is vital and intelligible. Not everyone likes it, to be sure, but no one need wonder what the artist is talking about.

STREET FIGHT OIL

Jessie Arms Botke

PEACOCKS AND CLUSIA   OIL

MANCHURIAN CRANES

Jessie Arms Botke

a painting career that has revolved around peacocks

JESSIE ARMS BOTKE fell in love with birds a good many years ago when she was a painter in the studio of Herter Looms of New York. The assignment to paint a peacock frieze for the dining room of Billie Burke's house at Hastings-on-Hudson was the event that started her on her unique and successful career. The design called for blue and white peacocks. "I didn't know there was such a thing as a white peacock," reminisced Mrs. Botke, "but I journeyed to the Bronx Zoo where I found one. It was love at first sight, a love that has inspired my brush ever since. It can truly be said that my entire career has revolved around peacocks. Now in my aviary at Santa Paula, California, I can enjoy and paint peacocks to my heart's content."

Those who have known Mrs. Botke's pictures throughout the years will be conscious of her predilection for white birds of various kinds—geese, ducks, pelicans and cockatoos, and the artist says that for a long time she painted only the white-feathered varieties. She found the white peacock especially appealing because of its simple and beautiful form. The texture

and pattern of the lacy tail, she explains, breaks the harshness of the white mass without losing the simplicity of the form. But, of course, Mrs. Botke no longer confines her interest to peacocks and white birds. In her own aviary she has blue peacocks, silver pheasants, golden pheasants, pigeons and ducks. But no cockatoos, because "you have to have steel wire to keep them in, they can cut chicken wire as if it were thread."

Mrs. Botke has devoted herself almost entirely to the painting of decorative bird pictures. She has haunted the zoos all over this country and Europe. She says, "I sketch in pencil, watercolor and oil. The most useful documents are those made in watercolor with white on gray paper. In that way I have accumulated very extensive records of all kinds of birds. In addition to sketching, I have made innumerable snapshots of specimens in the zoos in New York, Chicago, San Francisco, Paris and Amsterdam. In the Catalina Island aviary I have sketched for weeks at a time, and I have had the run of the San Diego cages. I have always preferred public collections," declares Mrs. Botke, "be-

JAVANESE OR GREEN PEACOCKS   OIL   40 x 32

SOUTH AMERICAN HERONS   OIL   24 x 20

cause the birds in them are so used to people milling around that they pay no attention to me when I am sketching, even when I draw inside the cages as I have done at Catalina."

It is obvious that Mrs. Botke has studied trees, plants and flowers as assiduously as she has studied birds. But she makes an interesting observation: "I learned long ago, that I shouldn't use the material until it 'cools off' and becomes more abstract in my mind, so that I can use it creatively rather than feel impelled to paint it as it looks realistically." Evidently her birds are subject to the same "screening" process because they are stylized and simplified to serve as decorative themes—and are thus saved from being merely reproductions.

Of course, it is the superb decorative quality of Mrs. Botke's work rather than its illustrative interest that accounts for the artist's reputation here and abroad. And it is interesting to note that she is at her best when her canvases contain two, or, at most, three birds. Those which include more individuals tend to sacrifice design to illustration. But these are in the minority. In most of her canvases she achieves her design by bold massing

of the birds and foliage forms. These are invariably enriched with fascinating detail which is so adroitly handled that it satisfies a natural desire for authenticity without impairing the simplicity of the composition. Her pictures combine the virtues of good design, meticulous detail and opulent color.

Mrs. Botke says that she does not make many preliminary notes or composition studies; she evolves the whole idea very completely in mind before she starts working. She says, "Sometimes I have a flow of ideas and start several canvases simultaneously, pictures that may not be finished for a year or two. Again, I may push one through to completion within a month. I prefer to work on a canvas until I am stumped, then set it aside and work on another until that reaches a dead end. Later I will return to them with an inspiration for their completion. I would like to be able to keep all of my pictures around until they cool off so I could judge them in a less prejudiced mood."

Regarding her painting methods, Mrs. Botke has this to say: "When painting in oil I have always liked to work on a hard surface, and I used to paint on canvas mounted on board or plywood. For the past ten years I have been painting on gesso grounds on presdwood, preparing the grounds myself.

"I draw the design in charcoal and pencil, and fix it lightly. Then paint with tempera, using a medium of one part egg yolk, one part damar varnish and two parts water. Over this I paint in oil. I like the gesso

NEST IN THE SIMSON WEEDS   OIL   32 x 40

ground because it is so perfect for gold leaf, which I like to incorporate in some of my color schemes. In underpainting with tempera, I use warm color where the final painting will be cool—such as ochre and sienna under green leaves and warm yellow under the white birds. The gold leaf is applied after the tempera and before the oil paint."

In recent years Mrs. Botke has also done a number of watercolors which, in contrast to her decorative oils, are very direct and realistic. She turned to watercolor as a relaxation from studio work and believes that this change of pace adds freshness and vitality to her oils when she returns to that medium. Several of these watercolors have received prizes in various exhibitions, including the California Water Color Show.

Jessie Arms Botke is the wife of Cornelis Botke, a native of Holland, who is well known as both painter and etcher. When the Botkes were married in 1915, recalls Jessie, "Many of my friends wagged sad heads over another lost art career. Still, it was our interest in art that drew us together and we have shared either the same studio or adjacent ones ever since. I early found that it was possible to be a homemaker and a mother and still keep up a working art career. But I did have to give up the regular feminine social round. Since all I really wanted to do was paint, it was no sacrifice.

"Artist teams are much more common now than they were when we were married," she points out, and adds without hesitation, "They work. I can't conceive of myself living with anyone but another artist. Cornelis and I lean heavily on each other for advice, criticism and encouragement. Our work is not at all alike, but when it comes to commissions such as murals and other large jobs, we can adjust ourselves to the other's style and do the orders as a team."

The Botkes are a comfortable pair who have not only made an art of living together as producing painters, but have even managed to combine fine art with farming. They raise apricots, vegetables and chickens on their ranch in a canyon near Santa Paula, California, where the air is hot and dry most of the year. And, like other farmers' wives around the country, Mrs. Botke does her own canning. Twenty dozen quarts of fruit are just part of the fun for this painter-grandmother (she has one son, two grandsons) who readily admits, "I love to cook. If life could be reduced to cooking and painting, it would be wonderful."

Mrs. Botke was born in Chicago. She was graduated from the Art Institute of Chicago, and followed this by study under John C. Johansen, Charles Woodbury and Albert Herter. Her work has won numerous prizes and honors and is in many museums and public collections.

Louis Bouché

PEPPERCOMBE   INTERIOR   OIL

14

Louis Bouché

a painter who has given up "art"

LOUIS BOUCHÉ was born in New York in 1896, but was taken as a boy to Paris where he enrolled in the Lycée Carnot, working also in the ateliers of Colarossi, La Grande Chaumière and L'École des Beaux Arts. When he returned to New York in 1915 he studied under Louis Mora and Frank Vincent Du Mond at the Art Students League. That same year he won the John Sanford Saltus Prize and Medal. In 1917 his work was included in the first New York Independents exhibition. Since then he has exhibited in leading national salons as well as in more intimate one-man shows.

There are, however, two strings to Bouché's art bow —easel and mural painting. The former, his first love, to no small extent has been made possible by profits from the latter. Back in 1922, Rodman Wanamaker asked him to start and run an art gallery in the New York store. "Of course," says the painter, "he was interested in everything French, and with the power of the store behind me all I had to do was to cable the Paris office and say: 'I want four paintings by Matisse and the latest Picassos.' I got them! I was given a free hand and we put on a lot of interesting shows and got plenty of publicity. Reginald Marsh first showed his pictures with us.

"We also did interior decorating. It was the era of the Florida boom, and Wanamaker's decorated almost all the big places down there. In fact, most of the leading decorators in New York today are graduates of that experience. Since I was a painter, it was up to me to suggest people to do murals. So I handed out plenty of lush plums to other artists over a period of some three years. Then I began to wonder why I couldn't do something of the sort myself. I quit the store in 1926 and for four years—until the depression killed it—ran my own mural painting business. It was just that. I worked for architects, decorators, and for the individual client as well, and I was grossing around $50,000 a year. That's a lot of painting! It was hack work, but I did it as honestly as I could. Most artists, I think, are honest and conscientious."

When the family cupboard begins to look bare Bouché still does a mural, and has to his credit decorations in the auditorium of the new Interior Building and in the hall of the Department of Justice Building in Washington, D. C.; in the Post Office in Ellenville, New York; and in four bar-lounge-cars of the Pennsylvania Railroad. In 1948, after two and a half years of work, he completed 115 feet of mural based on female "beauty" for the walls in the lobby of the cosmetic firm, Shulton, Inc., in its plant at Clifton, New Jersey.

Such big-scale work, however, is a far cry from the artist's easel pictures—those intimate flashes of daily experience that embrace everything from a dog and an automobile on a city street to an outdoor ball game, or his wife seated in the studio.

To understand how carefully Bouché sees and works out his painting even before he touches brush to canvas it is well to compare the oil, *Kingston Ferry,* with its preliminary pencil sketch. The drawing, done on the spot, records every detail of the picture down to the three-branched weed beside the tracks. A drawing of the man at the left was made on a separate sheet. He actually walked into the picture while Bouché was drawing, and he consented to stay put for a few moments until he had been sketched. His importance as pictorial support for the left side of the picture is appreciated when we cover him with a finger and see the resulting emptiness of the canvas at that point. It is interesting thus to discover how indispensable are those two white spots of the man's shirt and shoes as a balance for the white of the ferryboat.

As to color, we note with some surprise how meticulously the artist has followed the notations that appear on his penciled diagram, even such incidentals as the blue-gray roof of the little shanty against the red wall, and the ochre sand in the coal car.

This is Bouché's customary procedure, a quite unusual one. He goes to the appointed locale with his tracing pad (20 x 24), studies his subject and makes a careful diagrammatic drawing. Very rarely does he take his sketch box along; almost never does he paint his canvas on the spot. Back in his studio he proceeds to transfer the subject from drawing to canvas, by the squaring-up process, or tracing, if it is a facsimile.

He begins at once to work on his final painting without preliminary studies of any kind. If the work doesn't go to suit him there is always another canvas. Usually his preconceived composition satisfies him, though of course he does not hesitate to make changes as his picture develops. It is not unusual, however, for the final painting to follow his drawing and color specifications as faithfully as does *Kingston Ferry.*

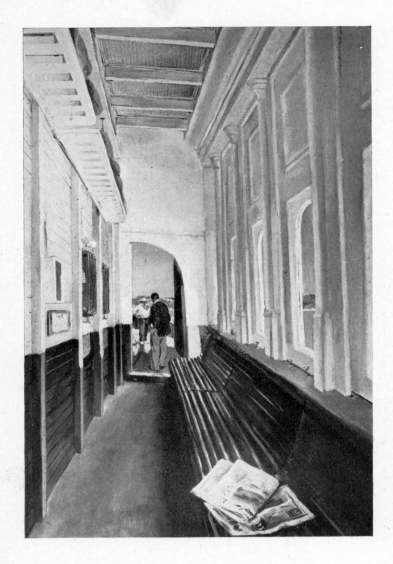

TEN CENTS A RIDE

OIL   45 x 30

Courtesy the Metropolitan Museum of Art

THE DOCUMENT

OIL   30 x 24

LONG ISLAND BALL GAME   OIL   20 x 26

When Bouché began to work on this picture, the boys gathered and watched over his shoulder. One asked, "Whatcha doin' that pitcher fur, the newspaper?" "No," replied Bouché, "I'm doing it for the Metropolitan Museum of Art." A few months later the painting was purchased by the Met.

A CORNER OF BOUCHÉ'S STUDIO

A careful pencil drawing of the subject is on the easel beside his painting. The squared-up lines, faintly visible on the drawing, indicate the artist's method of transferring the study from paper to canvas. Newspapers, cut to size and neatly stacked in the lower shelf of his painting cabinet, are used for cleaning brushes before they are dipped in the cleaning fluid or another color.

BELOW: An exact-size drawing of Bouché's largest and smallest brushes. The spread hairs of the bristle brush are deliberately splayed—as he is doing in the photograph below the drawing—because he likes that kind of brush.

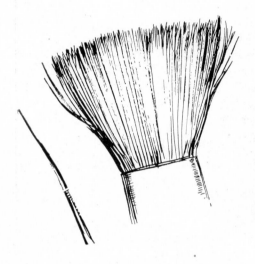

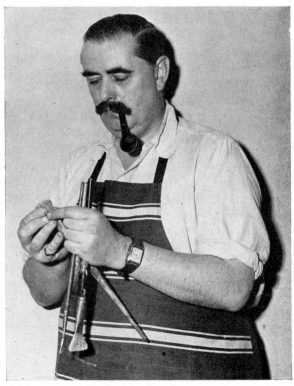

Bouché paints directly without underpainting of any kind, after he has carefully drawn-in the subject on his canvas. He begins by laying-in the neutral colors, and gradually works up to the more brilliant hues, of which there are few in his canvases though the general effect is rich and strong.

Bouché's paintings have won awards including a Guggenheim Fellowship for painting (1933) and the Carol H. Beck Gold Medal of the Pennsylvania Academy of the Fine Arts, 1944. Many of his canvases, also, have found their way into the nation's principal museums. The Metropolitan Museum of Art owns three. Bouché is represented at the Whitney Museum, Phillips Gallery, the Pennsylvania Academy of the Fine Arts, Cranbrook Museum, Worcester Museum, the Walker Art Center, University of Nebraska, Blandon Memorial Gallery, Museum of New Britain Institute, Wichita Museum, Encyclopaedia Britannica Collection, and American Academy of Arts and Letters.

Today, Bouché is an objective painter who is content to draw his inspiration directly from nature, viewing it, to be sure, in the spirit of his own mood or temperament, and revealing it through his fine sense of design and generally pleasing color.

This careful pencil drawing (20 x 24) with its written color notations is the exact size of the final painting, "Kingston Ferry." (See color reproduction.)

"Since I bought my country home," said Bouché, "I have come to realize how superb is the work of nature. It makes you truly religious! Nature is the great artist. I have lived too long and painted too much to feel that painting is everything. Love and living are more important. If you love, you love beauty and therefore you love nature. Unfortunately, many artists today get their biggest kick out of other people's art and don't go to the source of all great art—nature. Too much eclecticism inevitably leads to sterility. We are living in an arty period of good taste at any cost.

"Ten or twelve years ago I realized that I'd never set the world on fire. Like many others I worried all my life about producing 'art.' I was, you see, an esthete trying to produce beauty, but no amount of effort is going to do that because nature always does it so much better. So I just sat down in a simple way to paint the things I see. Now, I paint in a picture-postcard manner that is in conspicuous contrast to my Nottingham lace and abstract periods. Usually I put people in my canvases. Sometimes they are there when I begin; sometimes they just walk in. I find myself painting a little more directly from nature than I have done before."

After thirty-eight years of painting, Bouché feels that he has rounded a circle and is coming back to its start. "You know," he says from his experience as instructor at the Art Students League and at the New York School of Interior Decoration, "students often do remarkable things in the first six months, but it takes a long time for them to realize what made those things remarkable.

"I went through all sorts of phases. Painted abstract pictures years ago. Always admired Picasso. Probably have more books on Picasso than on any other master. I like his sense of humor and his ability to concoct. But if you put Picasso up against nature he turns out to be a second-rater. Look at the humor and fantasy in the shape of things we see all around us: bugs, plants, undersea life! Picasso can't touch nature's wit. But we owe Picasso and others of his ilk a lasting debt for jarring our too limited beauty standards. If it isn't a movie queen, a sunset, a baby or a kitten it isn't beautiful to most people. I don't believe God ever intended to play favorites in this manner—the endless variety of his creations attests to his love of all things living."

Roy Brown

CHANGE OF WEATHER COMING   OIL

Roy Brown

master painter of the American landscape

ROY BROWN is a painter who started his career with crystal clear vision. He knew what he wanted to do. He is an avowed disciple of tradition. All his life he has painted in that tradition, influenced by such eminent artists as Edward W. Redfield, Daniel Garber, Elmer Schofield, George Gardner Symonds and John F. Carlson, National Academicians, all of whom, as Homer Saint-Gaudens has neatly put it, "believe in interpreting the gracious side of life by way of sound technique."

Steadfastness of purpose has produced a consistent pattern in all of Brown's work. He has not deviated from his first youthful ambition to translate landscape with as much fidelity to its natural charm as is possible with paint on canvas. To attain this goal he painted most of his early canvases outdoors—summer and winter—in the *premier coup* method.

"In France," he confided, as we sat chatting in his New York studio, "I used to see Redfield going off to the country with a big 40 x 50 canvas and returning the same day with a completed picture. So I thought to myself, if he can do it why can't I? I found I could, and that my paintings got into the Salon with success."

But whether working directly in the field or more reflectively in the studio, what he has given us is a report of things seen by the physical eye. In him there is nothing of A. P. Ryder's mysticism. We could not think of Brown saying, as did Ryder: "Have you ever seen an inchworm crawl up a leaf or twig and there, clinging to the very end, revolve in the air, feeling for something, to reach something? That's like me. I am trying to find something out there beyond the place on which I have a footing."

Brown, to be sure, has done his groping but it has been for more power rather than for visions. He is the last man to be found wandering about in the murky realm of imagination. He is not at all a man of mood. He is designer rather than dreamer. He sees his landscape before him in bright light—each element clearly defined and playing its decorative part in a thoughtfully organized composition. He is master in this art of definitive orchestration. His pictures are never loosely put together, never casual.

Brown's pattern interest is as invariably expressed in his small sketches from nature as in his large canvases. It is interesting to note that his pencil insists, as does his brush, upon well-ordered arrangements, resolving the confusions of the landscape into a few simple planes. Few painters, I dare say, so completely anticipate their finished work in a tiny pencil study.

The outstanding characteristics of Roy Brown's painting are the flat, tapestry-like patterning of landscape forms and his technical vigor. He attacks his canvas with bold, direct strokes that seem to record his first intention. And these flat (in value) areas are alive with vibrant color. This is well demonstrated in the color reproduction of *The Little French Port,* one of Brown's smaller pictures.

Roy Brown has divided his time more or less evenly between Europe and New England. He was caught abroad by both World Wars, but, profiting by experience in the first, fled before the last could swamp him.

Returning steerage in World War I, with little money left in pocket, Brown landed in Silvermine, Connecticut, where he found an old abandoned mill beside a lovely little brook. As a habitation it looked hopeless—until his wife saw it. "The old New Englander who owned it thought we were crazy when we asked if he would rent it," the artist reminisced, "so we had to break down his resistance. He couldn't understand why anyone would want the place. Finally, however, he gave in and wanted to know whether we'd consider three dollars a month too much!

"The place had a huge space with eleven windows and two doors—a perfect studio, after I finished plastering it and my wife got busy with curtains and other details.

"All the time we were working on the mill I didn't lose a single painting day. And do you know," Brown chuckled, "when we left, the editor of *House and Garden* moved right in. That's what artists can do when they have ingenuity."

At heart Roy Brown is a trout-fishing, out-of-doors man. "Outdoors," he says, "you saturate yourself with what you see, and work with emotion while it's 'hot.' There's always the moment when you know you've got something. Then you hit and hit hard. After that you can't mess around."

Brown finds that he warms up to fine painting pitch much as a musician does through practice of scales and exercises. If he starts to paint in the spring he does his best work in August or September.

"When painting out of doors," he claims, "you get greater freshness and spontaneity; if it happens to be

Private collection

ALONG THE HARBOR   OIL   40 x 50

winter you take only time to establish the values and color before the cold stops you; the painting is rough, but the work is vital. Outside one can do in fifteen minutes what might drag out for three days in the studio. This working indoors requires sustained emotion, which is difficult to keep and at the same time retain the freshness of the outdoor spirit."

Brown is partial to a palette knife in laying oil paint on canvas. "When I use brushes," he says, "they are big ones, and are made of hog's hair bristle. I use the same sort of brush for watercolors. You can chisel right down to the paper with it. I don't like soft brushes."

As for his painting procedure he prefers to let his brush talk for him. "If someone asks me how I paint," he insists, "I honestly can't say. Things happen in the middle of a picture and you do what you never did before. Of course there are plenty of problems. Contrasts of line, of mass, of color and of value, for instance. I try out contrasts in my own pictures and sometimes they don't hold up. You can tell a student how to do it in twenty minutes, but it will take him twenty years before he knows what you are talking about. That's the disheartening part about creative work. You get a prize and it gives you a big lift. You say to yourself, 'Now

These experiments in composition demonstrate Roy Brown's interest in pattern, and his care in designing his subject so as to achieve the most telling presentation of it.

These pencil sketches from nature, reproduced here at about one-half size, reveal the same characteristics that distinguish Roy Brown's pictures—a superb sense of design, vigorous handling and good taste.

SOUHEGAN VALLEY   OIL   40 x 50

I've got it!' but you find out that your art graph goes on acting like the stock market—both up and down. Your brain doesn't always synchronize with your hand. But when hand and brain do hit together then you've really got something. And what's law for one painter may be suicide for another. Every painter is different. I look at another man's work and think to myself I can't paint the way he does, but I like it."

Although Brown works both in oil and in watercolor he has been a special champion of the latter medium, and is responsible for establishing a special watercolor section in the National Academy of Design. He served the American Water Color Society as its president from 1939 to 1949, resigning the position to assume the first vice-presidency of the National Academy.

His first real recognition dates back to 1915 when his painting of the dunes at Trepied, France, was purchased by the Friends of American Art for the permanent collection of the Art Institute of Chicago. Since then he has won many prizes including those of the Salmagundi Club, the National Academy (Altman Prize), Baltimore Water Color Club (Samuel J. Shaw Prize), National Arts Club and American Water Color Society. He is represented in the collections of the Metropolitan Museum of Art, Northwestern University, Springfield (Illinois) Art Association, National Arts Club, Hackley Gallery, Milwaukee Art Institute, John Herron Art Institute and Decatur Art Institute.

Roy Brown was born in Decatur, Illinois, in 1879. He received his training at the Art Students League with Kenyon Cox and George Bridgeman, and in Paris under John Paul Laurens, Rafaelli and Menard.

James Chapin

VIOLA PLAYER   OIL

James Chapin

profound painter of people and life

ANY consideration of James Chapin's art must of necessity focus first of all upon five momentous years of his life, beginning in 1924. His work, born of that period, profoundly influences other painters and, to a considerable extent, it influences our whole attitude toward contemporary art.

Before that time, American painting was pretty largely a reflection of the brilliant School of Paris. Almost every artist bowed down before the great god Cézanne, as indeed did Chapin himself. Painters tried to be as much like Picasso, Derain, Gauguin and Matisse as they could and dared. They were so wholly hypnotized by the work of these masters that they could not really see the form and color of their own native land. Chapin, who went from preliminary training at the Art Students League to study abroad, was part of all this postimpressionist enthusiasm; he did his share of experimenting with the various ultra-subjective schools of French Modernism.

Then came, as Grant Wood has put it, "the conquest of James Chapin by the Marvins." It is "one of the greatest stories of modern American art."

It came about because Chapin was broke and had to live cheaply in order to keep on painting. He journeyed to a rural countryside in northwestern New Jersey—not far from the scene of his boyhood days—where he found and rented, for four dollars a month, a two-room log cabin on the farm of the Marvins, a primitive, hard-bitten family. Chapin became so absorbed in spare, taciturn, unschooled Emmet, George and Ella Marvin that soon he found himself completely reoriented. The spirit of that bleak American farm and its inhabitants crept into his soul and wholly eclipsed his preoccupation with fashionable painting formulas.

The Marvins, at first suspicious, would not pose for Chapin; but they thawed out when he went to the fields to work with them, helped them plant potatoes, round up the pigs, and sat with the family around the kitchen stove in the evenings.

For five years he lived in almost complete isolation among the Jersey hills. Constantly he sketched and painted the Marvins at their work and in repose. He brought back a group of pictures which Grant Wood, writing in the catalogue of Chapin's 1940 New York exhibition, appraised as "among the best things in American art, strong and solid as boulders, . . . have established Chapin in the front rank of American painters." Of this same exhibition Edward Alden Jewell, *New York Times* critic, declared: "This show . . . establishes his position as second to none in our contemporary roster. It contains some of the finest paintings of our time." Other critics wrote in similar acclaim. From an obscure artist, Chapin had arisen to fame as the discoverer of the American scene long before the spotlight was turned on Curry, Benton and Wood. Some of the paintings of the Marvin saga now hang in the Art Institute of Chicago, the Pennsylvania Academy of the Fine Arts, Duncan Phillips Memorial Gallery in Washington, D.C., and the John Herron Art Institute, Indianapolis, Indiana.

Since the Marvin period, Chapin's brush has been busy with various aspects of the American scene. He has painted prize fighters, fishermen, baseball players, railway workers, blues singers and East Side life. He has also painted many distinguished portraits.

"As time passes," he says, "I find myself becoming more and more the painter of people, and also I find myself reaching more deeply for those symbolic human manifestations beyond the realm of individual likeness, or, rather, underlying it, that are common to mankind—the common structure, the immemorial gesture, the repeated yet ever fluid relationships of people in their own environments.

"Since this feeling has, I do believe, always informed what might be termed true portraiture, it has naturally followed that I have continued to paint some portraits. Among the more recent are those of Colby Chester, president of General Foods Corporation, now hanging in the New York Board Room of that organization, Mrs. Edwin Webster, Jr., Mrs. Russell Ziegler, Miss Helen Morgan, and the children of Mr. and Mrs. Philip M. Davis and Mr. and Mrs. John P. Marquand.

"My figure painting," Chapin continues, "also has taken on more of the aspect of portraiture, although in a more generalized sense. When a painting of mine entitled *Railroad Workers*—three railroad men grouped before a background of steam-engine forms—was chosen to be reproduced in the magazine *Voice of*

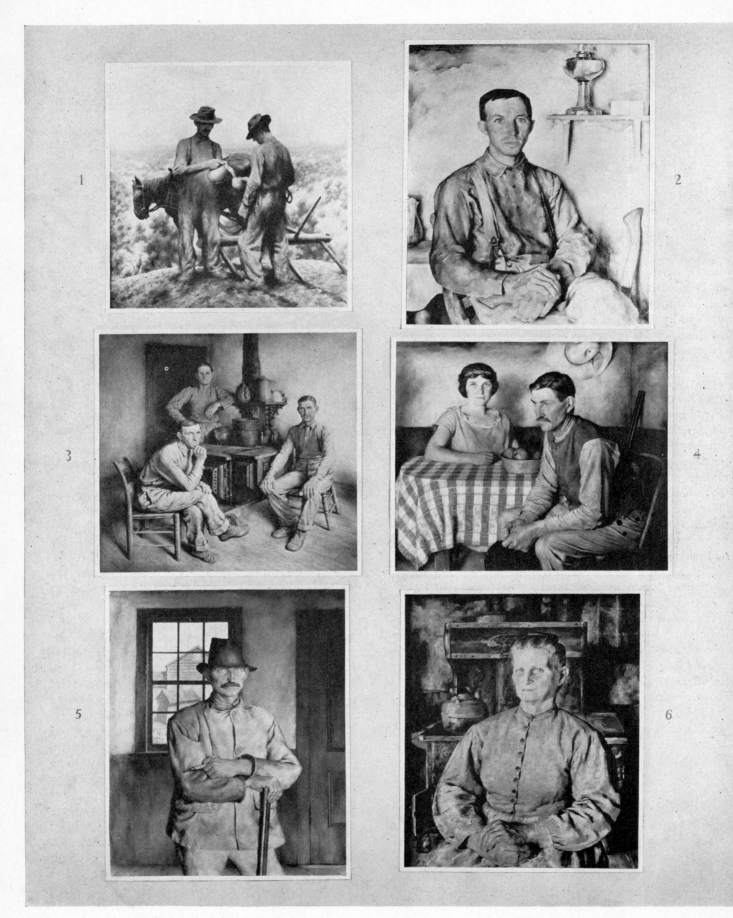

A GROUP OF CANVASES PAINTED BY CHAPIN DURING HIS "MARVIN" PERIOD

1. Time for a Drink, 2. Emmet Marvin, Farmer, 3. Emmet, George and Ella Marvin,
4. George Marvin and His Daughter, Edith, 5. Fox Hunter, 6. Miss Ella Marvin.

America, which has global distribution, I was gratified deeply, as I felt it meant recognition for a phase of my work heretofore not given such consideration."

How Does Chapin Paint?

As to technique there is little to report beyond the fact that he works in the direct method which was common to all contemporary painters, prior to the comparatively recent revival of the oil-tempera technique which involves underpainting in tempera with overglazing in oil colors, a method which does not appeal to Chapin.

In the development of ideas and composition Chapin is most deliberate and generally a slow painter. Some of his pictures have been in process for years. *Grindstone,* for example, was completed just seven years after it was begun. Some canvases mature quickly. It all depends upon how clear or how nebulous the first conception is, he explains. In spite of the fact that the impulse or inspiration to paint *Grindstone* was irresistible—otherwise it would have perished in the process—a satisfactory expression for it was attained only after persistent and repeated effort. You will note, for instance, in one of the early preliminary studies some farm sheds behind the figures, while in the finished picture the meadows stretch out to a distant village. The change had nothing to do with reasons of "atmosphere." It evolved as a result of the necessity for freeing the figures from the first too-close buildings which seemed to impair their movement. In a succession of experiments the buildings were pushed back until they disappeared and a distance emerged, a distance of rolling fields and hills built around curves, complementing the curve of the grindstone, the arch of the shadow on the ground, and the curves of the branch at the top of the picture. The very small town suggested in the middle-distance helps break the rolling movement there, which otherwise would be too smooth and monotonous. Furthermore, its small size, in perspective, adds to the illusion of space and gives the figures better scale.

In a portfolio in Chapin's studio I found dozens of sketches for *Grindstone* which somehow had managed to escape destruction. The few selected for reproduction give at least a hint of the exhaustive study that Chapin makes for every detail of a picture.

"In trying to discuss the painting of any particular canvas," Chapin says, "one can do little more than point out and attempt to explain obvious things in the picture itself, and perhaps hint at sources that are more or less subconscious and are sometimes so complex as to defy any attempt at analysis.

"With regard to the painting, *Grindstone,* the story content is immediately apparent. There is the act itself, the sharpening of the scythe blade, which has to do with the basic theme of harvestry. The New Jersey hill-farm environment determines to some extent the characteristics of the figures engaged, the types of faces, the heavy hands used to labor, the blue denim shirts faded by sweat and sun.

"But none of this 'story' or 'atmosphere' can be of more than passing interest to the artist until the circumstances of the action cause it to fall into relationships of form, color and line that inspire, by some chance of sight or thought, a formal pictorial structure, or what is commonly called a *composition.*

"Like most painters I begin work with a consideration of the larger space relationships: first of all with a feeling about the shape of the canvas and the sizes of figures and other objects within that shape. If the formal idea has been comparatively clear, these primary space relationships can sometimes be established in one or two sketches; if the mental image has been more or less nebulous—which is possible even though it be intensely *felt*—it must be groped for through many trials.

"I like solid things," he continues, "so my composing inevitably is concerned with the organization of objects in space (this in contrast to a two-dimensional decorative approach), objects constructed to symbolize their weight, and each related to every other object and the entire pictorial structure. In *Grindstone,* for instance (one example will suffice), the arms obviously form a sort of interlocking rhythm of their own, yet the directions they take and the means used to express them (color, contours, shapes of planes) carry on into and permeate the men's bodies, the grindstone and its carriage, the earth forms, the rail fence, the scythe and to some extent the entire canvas."

It will be seen from the above and from Chapin's innumerable pencil studies that there is nothing casual in his pictures. While he maintains that his approach to composition is through feeling rather than conscious structural analysis, it is certain that he subjects his canvases to the most exacting analysis as they progress.

If we put tracing paper over *Grindstone* and make an analysis of essential lines, we shall discover that it "works." It has a structure built up of carefully planned rhythms, harmonies, thrusts and counterthrusts. Every detail has pattern significance and, like small parts in a great machine, plays a vital role in the integration of the over-all design. We note, for example, the many studies of the folds of a sleeve, a painstaking search for just the right expression of that detail.

The simile of the machine is not far-fetched when we are thinking of the picture's structure which certainly may be said to have a mechanical aspect. Indeed Webster in attempting to define a machine tells us that it is "any device consisting of two or more resistant, relatively constrained parts, which, by a certain predetermined inter-motion, may serve to transmit and modify force and motion so as to produce some given effect or to do some desired kind of work." Is not this (omitting the last clause) a fair description of what the painter attempts to achieve with line, mass, space and color?

What has been said about the structure of Chapin's subject pictures applies equally well to his portraits, and a glance at the pencil drawings made for the portrait of Colonel Shields shows the same kind of study.

GRINDSTONE OIL

Unless you are prepared to give James Chapin an adequate number of sittings, there is no use in asking him to paint your portrait. Chapin, it seems, insists that a portrait should be a picture. That is, in addition to the portrayal of character, the canvas should be endowed with qualities that make any picture a work of art; that make the portraits by Velazquez, Rembrandt, Giorgione great pictures long after their sitters have been forgotten. Most people who get themselves painted care nothing about this, if indeed they even think about it. So long as they are given a nice flattering likeness with the painter's signature in the lower right-hand corner, they have their heart's desire. Unfortunately that also is the ceiling of the second-rate portrait painter's ambition—and capacity. But let us hear Mr. Chapin's own views on the subject.

"Painting Colonel J. Franklin Shields, chairman of the Board of Trustees of Pennsylvania State College, provided what might be called a perfect opportunity for creative portraiture.

"I knew, before I began, just where in a room at the college the portrait was to hang, so that, as a picture, it could be composed for its appointed space and its surroundings, and the conception could take on some of the properties and importance of a mural.

"Since Colonel Shields is a busy man the sittings were arranged to take place in a room adjoining his office in Philadelphia, where he could conveniently drop in off and on during the day and not feel pressed to keep distant studio appointments. It was thus possible to maintain that relaxed and informal relationship between sitter and painter by which I set great store.

"The sittings, about thirty in number, extended over a period of two months. I like it this way, because I personally am not interested in the rapid impressionistic portrait.

"I prefer the searched portrait, which affords the chance and the time to become acquainted with the sitter, and time—besides that needed for actual painting—to watch for and jot down in sketches and in

OPPOSITE: *A few of many pencil studies for "Grindstone"*

PORTRAIT OF COLONEL J. FRANKLIN SHIELDS

memory those fleeting and revealing expressions, material for a final synthesis of characterization that can be poignant and informed with life. And quite logically this attitude, say in relation to the human head, implies processes of simplification and emphasis that identify it with the deeper abstract aspects of art.

"Of course it goes without saying that the portrait must be a picture which embodies those abstract qualities in its very structure. A glance at the Shields portrait will reveal the simplicity of the main structural conception—active angles and diagonals moving crosswise through arms, legs, shoulders, pipestem and inclined books are superimposed on a series of verticals and horizontals formed by the edges of the filing cabinet, carpet and baseboard, chair arms and desk. These verticals and horizontals find related echoes in the picture frame and picture on the wall.

"One might also point to the up-and-down movement of the curved directions extending from the chair-arm support up through the coat lapels and necktie into the light and shadow division of the head, where it is resolved, although it also has its echoes in the slightly emphasized curves of the tree branches in the picture.

"It seemed best to modify the severity of their structural direction passing through the head by way of cheek and temple, by bringing the half-shadows from a slightly smiling mouth to meet and slightly break it. So, many swift sketches of the head were made during moments of conversation, and muscular changes searched for and noted.

"I suppose it would be possible to carry this kind of analysis very far if one were to discuss at length the more subtle relationships involved in painting, the

OPPOSITE: *Pencil studies made for the portrait of Colonel Shields*

32

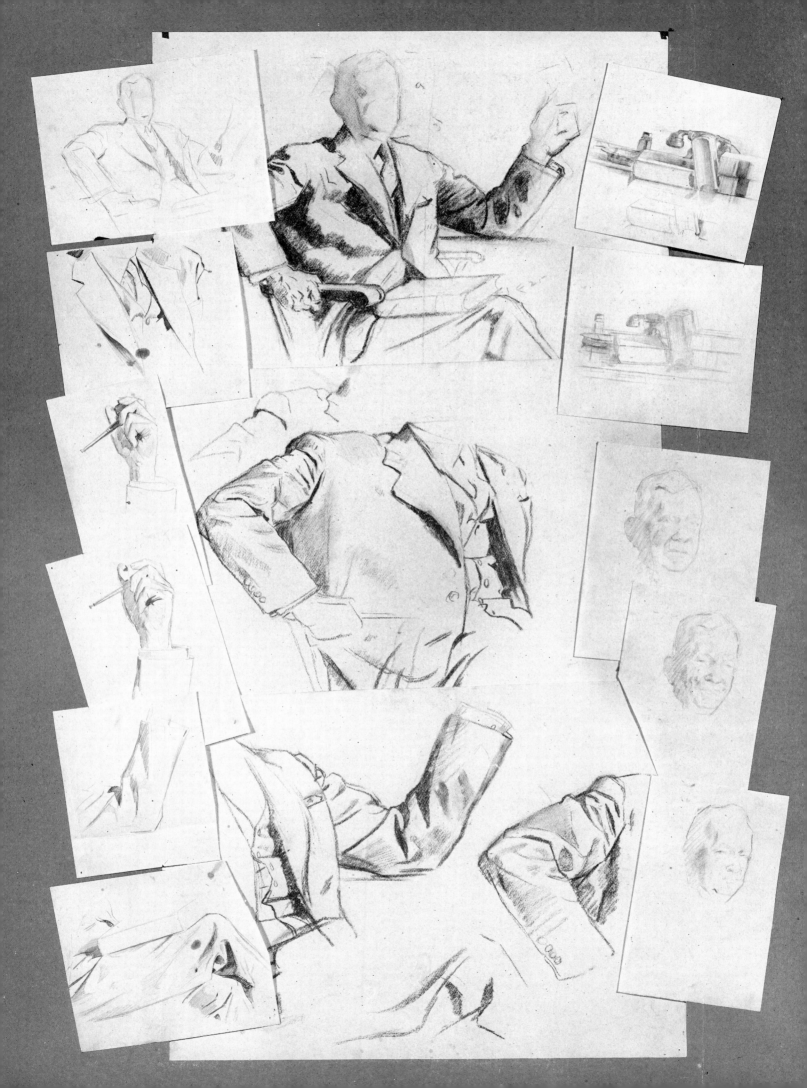

wheels within wheels. There would be the matter of color, of plastic surfaces, of simplification of form or of its significant embellishment, of intervals which have to do with rhythm as surely as do intervals between sounds in music—and so on deeper and deeper into a maze of rationalization after the fact, a province the artist might better leave to the critic."

Born in West Orange, New Jersey, in 1887, Chapin has found in the hill country of his native state the material most congenial to his mature brush. Married in California in 1941 (he now has two little boys), he left New York's Greenwich Village "for good" in 1946 to make his home in Glen Gardner, New Jersey, where he bought an old farm, converted the barn into a studio, and turned his back not only on New York but also on teaching. For several years he had lectured at the Pennsylvania Academy of the Fine Arts, and during the summer, with Millard Sheets, taught in the Fine Arts Department of Claremont Colleges, California.

"I really gave up all teaching in 1945," Chapin told us, "in order to devote myself exclusively to my own work. Here in my barn-studio I spend most of the day painting, although in the late afternoon there are jobs to do around the place—wood to be cut, vegetable garden to be made and tended in season, and masonry repairs to be made to our stone buildings. I do enjoy cementing stones together!"

Chapin has been honored by awards from the Pennsylvania Academy of the Fine Arts, the Carnegie Institute and the Art Institute of Chicago, and he tells an amusing story about two prizes that seemed to sum up the reaction to his art of the man-in-the-street. One year when he exhibited at the Detroit Art Institute, he won its "unpopular prize" for a symbolic picture, *Hymn to Earth;* while, not long thereafter, the public voted him the popular prize at the Carnegie Institute for his portrait trio *Emmet, George and Ella Marvin* around their kitchen stove.

His work has found its way into such permanent collections as those of the Art Association of Indianapolis, the Newark Museum, Amherst College, Abbott Laboratories and the Encyclopaedia Britannica.

John Costigan

STUDY OF A CALF   LITHOGRAPHIC PENCIL

John Costigan
the Millet of American painting

Two museum directors were examining John Costigan's paintings in a New York gallery. One, turning to the other said, "I think it is quite appropriate to call Costigan the Millet of American painting today."

After the day which I recently spent with John Costigan in his rural home, the same thought occurred to me quite forcibly. It was not until I had written what follows that I learned, from Carmine Dalesio, director of the Babcock Galleries, that this reference to the Barbizon painter had been made long ago in his establishment.

It is easy to think of Orangeburg, New York, as Costigan's Barbizon and the lovely woodland that borders Hackensack Creek as his "Fontainebleau." For throughout the twenty-eight years of Costigan's residence in Orangeburg, he has painted just about all of his pictures in his peaceful little "forest." Like Millet he has pictured the quiet beauty of rural life, the everyday happenings of life on the farm, sunlight and shadow in the woods. Like Millet he invites us to the peace of isolated pastoral existence.

Costigan's message, unlike Millet's, is essentially a song of joy, a testimony to the fulfillment of good family life on the farm. He shows us the felicities rather than the fatigues of farm life. He is obsessed by the renewal of life in his children and their companionship with the ewes and lambs, the cows and calves, that represent nature's regeneration. On Costigan's canvases his children are born and grow up, happy in

the blessing of healthy outdoor living. They romp with the goats and disport themselves like wood nymphs among the trees and in the stream where their glistening bodies have been their father's inspiration and subject matter throughout the years.

There has been no dearth of models in the Costigan menage, no need to seek them beyond the family group. There are five children—two boys and three girls—and now, the youngest being sixteen, their places are taken by two grandchildren, Danny, five, and Susie, three. These, the grandfather paints with the same enthusiasm as was lavished upon his own. Until the grandchildren came along to confuse matters, one could identify the chronology of Costigan's work by the youngsters in the picture.

Mrs. Costigan has been the painter's only model for the women who appear in his pictures. These women are invariably heavy and peasant-like, stolid and earthy, really quite unlike the artist's wife who, if not exactly slight, is by no means peasant-like.

As to the goats and the cow and the calves, they have disappeared from the Costigan acres.

I spoke of Costigan's message. Of course, he has no message in the propaganda sense; neither had Millet for that matter, although his work, in his day, was stigmatized as "socialistic." Every artist paints that which he loves and that which surrounds him. When Millet painted the pathos of the peasant on the land he only recorded the objective truth of what he saw. Because

FISHERMEN   WATERCOLOR   16 x 20

Private collection

the truth was in itself a social protest, his pictures were labeled "propaganda."

Of course we are more keenly aware of the painter's love of paint for paint's sake when, as with Costigan, the subject matter is felicitous. For almost thirty years Costigan has continued to paint the beauties of nature and the amenities of sheltered family life. His art has been untouched by the tragedies of the past decade. One would think he was unconcerned about all that goes on outside his little forest did we not know that he went overseas to fight in World War I. In his "Fontainebleau" the sun has continued to shine down through the trees upon the children at play; the pastoral peace has been undisturbed.

To be sure, sweetness and light is frowned upon in some quarters today and few critics dare call a picture beautiful. Well, Costigan has not been afraid of the kind of beauty that most intelligent people recognize and enjoy, nor have sixty-two museums which own his pictures. His is not sentimental beauty nor the beauty of nature as reproduced by kodachrome; it is such beauty as can only be realized by an artist of great sensitivity, creative power and unusual mastery of technical means.

If you go to visit Costigan you will be met by a tall, rather gaunt man topped by a thick mane of white hair. An early photograph depicts him as a somewhat fierce looking young man with piercing dark eyes. Now his eyes are kindly and patient, his mien friendly.

He will take you into his low-ceilinged studio which occupies most of the lower floor of his two-storied house. Facing the door as you enter is a tall, bulbous stove. On top is a vase of flowers, and below, last winter's ashes sift onto the unswept floor. To the left is an enormous etching press nearly hidden by a litter of papers and assorted studio junk. Books, magazines, jars and bottles, and piles of watercolors, prints and sketches fill shelves all around the room. Canvases and frames stand on the floor and out from the walls, crowding in upon the center of the room.

A battery of fluorescent lamps is attached to the ceiling just inside the door and in front of the stove. Under this light Costigan sets up his easel to paint and, when working in watercolor, lays his paper flat on a low table. Sometimes he stands, sometimes sits at his work.

On a low stand nearby is his watercolor palette—a white enameled laundry tub cover about two feet square. It is likely to be pretty well slopped up with color, as it was when I was there. Costigan says he washes it when it gets too bad. His oil palette is heavily encrusted with dried pigment and suggests the heavy impasto of his canvases.

John Costigan was born in 1888 in Providence, Rhode Island. Between 1902 and 1921 he lived in New York. During a part of this period he did theatrical posters and other commercial work. He is entirely self-taught, never having attended art school—except for a

This reproduction of a watercolor in an early stage of its development is characteristic of Costigan's approach to all his pictures, whether he is working in oil or watercolor.

SPRING LANDSCAPE WITH FIGURES   OIL   25 x 30

DEEP IN THE WOODS   OIL   30 x 36

FALL PLOWING   ETCHING   8 x 13

Costigan painting his children in Hackensack Creek bordering his Orangeburg acres.

Costigan readies his etching press.

Mr. and Mrs. Costigan pose with grandchildren, Danny and Susie.

Costigan paints a watercolor in his Orangeburg studio.

few weeks in the Art Students League. However, he had just about the best training possible for a painter. For years he drew from the model at the famous Kit Kat Club, a life class patronized by practicing illustrators and newspaper artists. Those years of evening sketching from the nude, without instruction, gave him the thorough knowledge of the figure which is the basis of the remarkable technical command seen in his impressionistic watercolor renderings of the figure.

This dexterity is especially impressive in his watercolors because in them one can see how he has expressed his knowledge in quick unaltered strokes of his brush which unfailingly define the form, register the color and create that sparkle of life so characteristic of his work in this medium. His command of the figure is so great that his painting, as you watch him work, seems automatic and wholly effortless. A sweep of the brush and there is an arm; a deft touch or two, an entire head. One has the feeling, the confidence, that the brush simply could not register a false note, just as in listening to a Rachmaninov recital one expects inevitable perfection of rendering.

Costigan is as much of a giant in the print world as in the realm of paint. He seems to be as much at home with the etcher's needle as with the brush. Indeed his power as a composer is especially evinced in this black-and-white medium. He gives us in an etching a complete symphony of line and tone color that contains the carrying quality of a fine painting. To the power and verve of painting he adds, with his etching needle, great sensitiveness of detail and fine line delineation. The subject here reproduced, one of his latest plates, clearly demonstrates this combination of qualities. Costigan's prints naturally have the habit of winning awards in the big print shows.

It is refreshing to find a painter who excels in different mediums. Costigan refutes the rather general opinion that no painter can achieve equal distinction in oil and in watercolor. There is a theory that an artist is by nature either a "dry" or "wet" worker—watercolor is a "dry" medium since it dries rapidly—and that he is unlikely to function equally well in the other medium which is "foreign" to his nature. Maurice Grosser maintains, in his *Painting in Public,* that

". . . if anybody, by some particular knack or uncommon virtuosity, manages to learn to paint in watercolor, all his watercolors will look just like the watercolors of everyone else. . . . And all his watercolors will be landscapes, because portraits and figures and still life are much too hard to do in that temperamental conglomeration of drip, sop and run. Worst of all, when a beginner has once learned to paint in watercolor he can never learn to paint in oil. He cannot train himself to be extravagant enough with his paint or time, or to paint with thick lights and thin darks which is more or less normal in oil and precisely the opposite to what one must do in watercolor." Grosser concludes by declaring that, "Consequently, it is very easy in any exhibition of oil paintings to spot the painters who have the habit of watercolor."

Well, perhaps Costigan does excel in watercolor— certainly there are few, if any, in America who match his performance in this medium—but his work in both mediums refutes all the dogmatisms of the above quotation. A Costigan watercolor seen in an exhibition dominates the wall. In originality of conception and in uniqueness of rendering it resembles no other watercolor ever painted. And one who has seen his oils is first of all impressed by their heavy impasto and remarkable facility in brush work. A characteristic Costigan canvas is heavily encrusted with pigment, sometimes a quarter of an inch or more thick. Hillocks of paint rise and fall as on a topographical map. Viewed at close range, it is likely to be unintelligible; but at a distance the confusion is resolved, and seeming abstract areas take their place in a brilliant and harmonious orchestration of color and form.

Costigan's oils, watercolors and prints have won a goodly share of the important prizes in these fields and he is represented in the nation's leading museums and collections, including the Metropolitan Museum, the Library of Congress, the Brooklyn Museum, Los Angeles County Museum, the Art Institute of Chicago and the Phillips Memorial Gallery. He has three murals to his credit, one in the Girard (Ohio) U. S. Post Office, one in Rensselaer (Indiana) U. S. Post Office and the other in the Post Office and Agricultural Building at Stuart, West Virginia.

Russell Cowles

ADAM AND EVE   OIL   40 x 50

Russell Cowles
one of America's most creative painters

Russell Cowles is a quiet-mannered man with a unique gift for clarity in thought and utterance. You sense at once that he is a person of all-round cultural attainments. You are not surprised to learn that while spending his life in painting he has at the same time spent it in exploring and considering the problems involved in art expression; that he won the coveted Prix de Rome and lived in Italy for five years as a Fellow of the American Academy in Rome; and that, still exploring the field of art, he journeyed to China, Japan, Egypt and Greece. That, plus his art study at the National Academy of Design, the Art Students League, and a year or more in Paris, is his training background.

The years in Rome appear to have been truly constructive. That is not always the experience of Prix de Rome men. So often the dead hand of classicism has lain too heavily upon the shoulders of young aspirants ever to be shaken off. But Cowles somehow was able to receive the Academy's blessings while resisting its hypnotic authority. Indeed, he calls his Rome experience one of the richest of his life, but adds, paradoxically, that it took ten years to get over the effects of it.

At any rate he has emerged—as he must have entered—an original, creative man; a profound student of art and of life, with the rare ability of expressing *both* in his environment as well as in his pictures.

In the remodeling and decorating of his century-old stone house in New Milford, Connecticut, for example, he has revealed his extraordinary good taste. In the building of his huge timbered studio he has displayed a considerable knowledge of architecture. His craftsmanship is seen in several fine pieces of furniture that he has designed and constructed.

These "applied arts" attainments may seem to have little to do with Russell Cowles' accomplishment as a painter, but I think they do in fact have significance as background in the study of a man whose progress has been marked by unusually orderly and logical development. In my opinion, a man of such completeness is likely to have an especially trustworthy vision of his work in relation to the world in which he lives.

It is not my purpose to present an extensive outline of Russell Cowles' career, instructive as that might be. All I shall attempt is to record some of the impressions I gleaned in my visit to his studio.

On his easel, at the time, was the start of a second version of *Adam and Eve,* different in some essentials from the first painting of that subject, shown here in halftone, yet designed upon the same general plan. Three small studies, two in oil and one in pastel, represented the preliminary study for his final 40 x 50 canvas. These two Adam and Eve pictures and a few others constituted a new "period" in the evolution of Cowles' painting philosophy.

This phase is characterized by (1) a stronger sense of the picture plane and (2) a color approach in flat masses which almost ignores light and shade. Each of these two viewpoints presupposes the other for, as Cowles says, "When you paint in flat color areas you seek a color equivalent for modeling, achieving the necessary definition of form through line. And lines, defining contours, even in the distance, tend to pull everything back to the surface of the canvas. Lines may also play an added role in enriching and emphasizing the rhythmic pattern of the picture. In an abstract sense, you are playing flat color areas against a pattern of line."

If you will study the *Adam and Eve* pictured here, Cowles' meaning should be clear even though color is lacking in the reproduction. Note the outlines freely used throughout and the extremely flat painting of the principal color areas. "Modeling by means of light and shade, in the traditional method of painting," says Cowles, "tends to break up a picture so that objects are in danger of becoming too important, impairing the concept of the picture as a whole, as well as destroying the simplicity and effectiveness of the color areas."

This is no new theory, as we all know. Cézanne spent an entire lifetime experimenting with deep space through color relationships, with strict regard for the picture plane, that is, the surface of the canvas. This philosophy is opposed to the ideal of space as expressed through three-dimensional modeling, the sculptural concept. "The modern painter," explains Cowles, "creates a sense of deep space by superimposing one color area upon another, with interrelated and interlocking

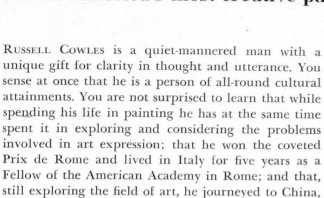

WEB OF NIGHT 1947 OIL 40 x 50

On these pages we see how Russell Cowles' concepts of pictorial statement have varied during the past decade

QUANDARY 1941 OIL 34 x 24

shapes. When this is successful he achieves total picture space even though individual objects be as flat and two-dimensional as theatre scenery. Of course they should not give the beholder such an impression, but should take on a feeling of solidity by color and placement."

Continuing, "Whether painting is called a visual art because it represents something seen or, as our modern friends would perhaps prefer, because it is something to be seen, it is in any case an arrangement of colored shapes on a flat surface. How these colored shapes relate to the world of reality and what effect they have because of their particular pattern on the eye and mind of the beholder, that is the whole problem.

"I have said that these colored shapes are arranged on a flat surface. If that were all, I would take an adjective from this word 'surface,' and describe the effect as superficial, which is at once the limitation and the possible charm of what is commonly called, or damned, by the word 'decorative.'

"I referred a moment ago to the relation of these colored shapes to the world of reality. This real world is three-dimensional in contradistinction to our picture surface which is two-dimensional. It is the space of astronomy, physics, solid geometry. Now to a painter *space is the matrix of reality*. The control, the manipulation, the organization of space in relation to the picture surface lies at the heart of the art of painting. This I must assert categorically. Should a painter deny it he would thereby class himself as either a decorator or an illustrator, the former thinking only of the picture plane, the latter forgetting its existence.

"This discipline of space underlies all great painting from the Chinese masters of T'ang and Sung, to Giotto, to El Greco, to Cézanne. It does not endeavor to realize on the canvas the three-dimensional or 'deep' space of the physical world. Such imitative painting, where the frame is like an open window onto the world outside, eats away the picture surface. The aim, on the contrary, is to preserve this surface. Art is all a matter of relations, and in this instance it is the relation of 'deep space' to the canvas surface. It is a paradox.

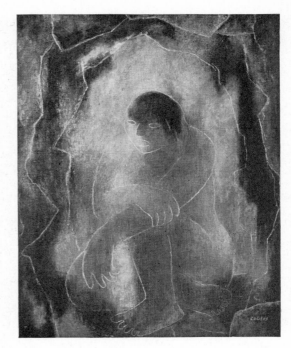

THE FARMER'S DAUGHTER 1948 30 x 24

BEFORE EVE WAS LILITH 1948

"Deep space," as Cowles has said, "is mystical. It can be achieved," he declares, "through light and shade, the approach of Rembrandt and El Greco. Or by color, as in the work of Cézanne and Matisse. Combine both approaches and you achieve vulgarity. A painter must decide what direction he will take; he cannot go two or three different ways at the same time. His choice is an outcome of his spirit and his work, but whatever his choice, something must be sacrificed. Monet, for example, sacrificed form for the sake of light. All great style stems from economy of means.

"There is a saying," Cowles continued, "to the effect that you don't like a thing because it's good—it's good because you like it. Many systems of esthetics have probably been little else than a rationalization of this notion. Some people don't like the color magenta, others don't like garlic in their salad dressing. Your likes and dislikes are very important to you, but this does not give them a general validity. And your preferences may change with increasing experience. At any rate, the fact that you prefer blondes, for instance, does not justify your advocating that all brunettes be put to death.

"This holds true in the field of art. So keep an open mind, if you can, and when in doubt learn to suspend judgment. You can sometimes gain as much, perhaps, from painting you don't like as from that you do, maybe more. When I was a young painter, I was too inclined to close my mind to painting I didn't like. Today I am very fond of some of that painting.

"On the other hand, you may be different. You perhaps have an open mind, and a confused one. Confronted with all the welter of styles, the different schools of painting that flourish or languish around us, you

may ask yourself what you *ought* to like. This is because your artistic character is in process of developing, and time alone will enable you to pick out your ultimate path.

"If I were asked to advise a young painter starting out on his career, I should say to him: 'Even as a beginning art student you probably surpassed the average person in manual dexterity, and haven't had too much difficulty in mastering the handling of your materials or in making your hand obey the dictates of your eye and mind. The real question is: how well trained are your eye and mind? Just as a student of the violin cannot make much progress until he can detect the most delicate differences of pitch, volume and time interval, so you will grow in stature as a painter only as you refine your discrimination of color values, color relations, and so on. You no doubt know a good deal about perspective and anatomy. You can draw, in a sense, in that you can represent an object in its volume, its light and shade, its general character. Whether your drawing has much style, however, whether your line is sensitive, expressive, is perhaps more doubtful. When you have made some progress along these lines, when you know something about the structure of a painting, and particularly when you feel more or less at home in the matter of color organization, and finally, space organization, then you will be justified perhaps in considering yourself an artist.

'The business of color is complicated. While it is probable that the supreme masters of color are "born that way," I am certain that whatever native gift they may have has been developed through training. Our painters seem to me to submit willingly to self-discipline in drawing, composition, organization of their

47

BLUE NIGHT   1946   OIL   22 x 28

CONNECTICUT FARM   1940   OIL   32 x 40
This canvas was underpainted in tempera.

48

BLUE HERON 1945 OIL 20 x 30

pictures in light and dark balance, but to leave the matter of color to feeling or "instinct." The result is usually accidental or capricious.

'Of course if you are a "primitive" or wish to be one, then not only color but all the other elements in your work will remain undisciplined. But good primitive painting is rare, even on the level of quaintness and charm, and the added gift of intuitive grasp of structure and organization is extremely rare.

'If, then, you decide to train yourself as an artist I see no reason why your use of color should be the one anarchistic element in your work. Emphasizing again the prime necessity of developing the greatest possible sensibility of the eye, without which no system or theory of color will do you any good, and disclaiming any interest in color systems, good or bad, I still think that certain things about color, the result of long experience by many artists, can be stated for your benefit.

'Perhaps the first of these is the balance of cool and warm colors. Cool and warm are relative terms. A neutral gray alongside a hot red will feel cool, while the same gray next to a cold blue will feel warm. Neutral tones, incidentally, are extremely important. So much so in fact that a fine colorist can almost be distinguished by the way he uses neutrals in modifying and balancing his strong colors.

'Next in importance might be the use of a dominant color. Everybody knows the old gag of what would happen if an irresistible force met an immovable body. The answer can be found in most any large art exhibit. When a picture contains two opposing colors, each in its fullest intensity, and of relatively equal quantity and importance, a conflict occurs that must destroy the unity of the picture in spite of anything the painter can do about it. The answer is that one color should dominate the others, just as one form in a composition must dominate the rest. A saturated color in a small area may balance a large area of another less saturated color in a way that does not destroy the picture unity. Two opposing colors that clash when adjacent to each other often live happily in the same picture when separated by a neutral area. Strongly opposing colors set up a tension between them, and such tensions should not occur in haphazard fashion in a picture, but should be reserved for the occasions when needed.

'Color can be used for its shock value, and often is so used, though frequently at the expense of other, more durable qualities. But when employed knowingly and intelligently it can be very effective. Perhaps the greatest color shock comes from the combination of intense red and intense green. It is widely used by our American painters, rarely by Europeans. If it is a national characteristitc, I hope it will eventually be outgrown. Surely there are other and better ways in which our national temperament can find expression.

'To get the most benefit from the study of color and to develop a sense of color organization, I think it is very desirable to experiment with the plan of starting a picture in color, rather than taking up the color question after drawing and composition have been determined. For such experimentation I would suggest employing a set palette. That is, pick out three, four, or five colors that seem interesting together, add one or more neutrals—grays for a more quiet effect, black and white (to be used pure) for a more exciting result—and plan to compose the picture with these elements only. Decide at the beginning which is to be the dominant color, and stick to your decision. Then perhaps try another sketch with the same palette, but choosing one of the other colors as the dominant.

'When modern painting is attacked for failing to express certain things, such as the aspect of things as they might appear in a color photograph, for instance, its defenders often content themselves by replying that such was not its intention. Which of course is true, as you no doubt know. What you should also know is what its intention *is*. Until you do, you can hardly have an intelligent opinion about it. The most frequent criticism leveled against modern painters is their distorted drawing. Objects, figures, are pulled out of their natural shape, or compressed, in the interest of design, or pattern, or for heightened expressiveness. But in many cases it is really space which is distorted for these reasons, and the objects get distorted by the distorted space. For this thing that interests painters so much, namely space, cannot be expressed or represented directly, but only by means of objects which exist in it, delimit and define it. Much of a painter's apparent concern with objects, their placement, volume, and relation to other objects, is really a concern with space relations, which these objects reveal and express. And the freer a painter is in searching for psychological truth as against the obvious factual truth of photography, the farther he will go in allowing his manipulations of space relations to involve a concomitant distortion of the objects.

'Of course there are many painters who do not go this far, who play with space relations without doing much or any violence to the natural appearance of objects. In many of the paintings of Salvador Dali, or the early Chirico, space is stretched out in depth, creating an almost unbearable feeling of nostalgic solitude and melancholy. In the cubist paintings of Picasso and Braque space is contracted. It is contracted, telescoped, in its third dimension, depth, to a matter of a few inches, while at the same time it is often condensed in its two-dimensional design, resulting in a compactness that heightens the intensity of its pattern, and creates another kind of feeling, to which, in the case of these painters, the accompanying distortion of forms contributes.

'Aside from surrealism, most ultramodern painting contracts its third dimension, depth, almost out of existence. I say "almost" because with the best men of this school it is a case of extreme condensation, and *not* elimination. They want the subject, the content of their painting, to become identified completely with the physical canvas, and to do this they try to relate all depth sense to the picture plane. The picture plane is their frame of reference, and must be felt at all times in conjunction with the sensation of depth. Each area of their picture, each color, shape, tone, plays a dual role, existing both on the picture plane and back of it in space.

'It is possible,' I would say, in conclusion, to the young painter, 'that the extreme modernists carry this business too far, that their insistence on the importance of the picture plane becomes an obsession. But in any case they have opened up a new field for painting, enlarged the range of art expression. I merely wish to suggest that you, instead of making a premature judgment, then closing your eyes and your mind to what you don't like, whether old or new, try to grasp the implications of the different approaches to the space problem, and to develop your sensibilities to such a point that you can understand and appreciate some of the deeper significance of what art is about.' "

Cowles himself is not a man to jump impulsively from one "style" to another for the sake of being up to date. His progress is by evolution, not revolution. You can be certain that whatever looks new in his work has been incubating inside for a long time. His is a deliberate spirit.

But Cowles does not consider art primarily an intellectual procedure. "It is altogether an expression of the spirit," he will tell you, "and intuition is the chief guide when it comes to the actual painting. The intellectual contemplation takes place in between times and serves to clarify the issues involved."

Russell Cowles' interests encompass a wide variety of subject matter. In addition to landscape, he has painted portraits, nudes, anecdotal genre and animals. He is an impeccable draftsman. In his nature painting he has never been content to copy nature. "Nature," he says, "is ever full of hints, but indeterminate and indecisive. That is nature's charm; she leaves the job to the artist so that his painting is an exchange between him and nature. His canvas should be *his* work of art."

Since, today, Cowles' approach to painting is through color rather than black and white, he does not resort to monochromatic underpainting which, he says, is especially adapted to the sculptural concept of form. For the same reason, he uses charcoal less and pastel more for preliminary studies.

When it comes to "good painting," Russell Cowles is a traditionalist. He insists that underlying the swift processing of fashions in art, of changes in style or content, there must always remain the tradition of good painting. "Good painting," says Cowles, "means discipline as well as eager enthusiasm. It is not a stunt."

Francis de Erdely

WOMAN WITH SHOVEL   DRAWING   30 x 22

Francis de Erdely

a painter of great perception and power

FRANCIS DE ERDELY, Hungarian-born artist, is one of the most creative painters working in America. He first achieved prominence in Hungary where, in Budapest, he won the Szinyei-Merse Grand Prize in 1925, then became well-known in Spain, Holland, Belgium, (Triennial Bronze Medal at Ghent, 1929) France, Czechoslovakia and Australia. His work has been commissioned or bought by the former Queen Mother of Spain, Maria Christina, the late Prince Hendrik of Holland and, of later years, by American museums and collectors. He has received resounding praise from critics, and has won a total of 27 prizes in America since 1940—nine of these in 1949. Few contemporaries have been honored by an accolade such as that conferred by Arthur Millier in the Los Angeles *Times*. Writing about De Erdely's Los Angeles exhibition in 1944, Millier said, "Impressive as the 29 paintings are, the show reaches its climax in 14 large black-and-white drawings of the horrors of war which are worthy to stand with Goya's famed *Disasters of War* etchings." Alfred Frankenstein in the San Francisco *Chronicle* voiced his similar conviction that "they are among the most powerful drawings you will ever see."

It has been my privilege to see a score or more of these drawings. They are large—almost 30 inches high, as I recall—and are done with various mediums: woodstick and india ink, conte crayon, brown pastel and wash. They are indeed impressive; some, like *Woman with Shovel,* which we reproduce, have an epic quality. Does it not remind us of Millet's peasants, especially *The Man With the Hoe?*

Frankenstein, remarking that De Erdely was once a professional boxer, says, "Perhaps that has something to do with the power and palpability of his figures. Innumerable artists have studied athletes in action; one who has himself been an active athlete may have an edge, so far as knowing the thrusts and articulations of

the human body is concerned." At any rate, De Erdely is a master anatomist and his drawings, to resort to ringside jargon, pack a terrific punch.

De Erdely paints as he draws, in what today is considered large scale. His "small" canvases are 24 x 30 or, more often, 30 x 40. He says, "To paint on a really small scale would present, to me, the baffling situation of both clarifying a problem and simultaneously subduing it."

But De Erdely's canvases have a bigness that is independent of size; their monumental quality is as obvious in small reproductions as in the originals. One is not surprised to learn that the composition of his pictures is the result of prolonged study and development before brush is touched to canvas. More than a hint of his creative processes may be gleaned from the reproductions of a few of his study documents for *Day's End,* and from his own description of his procedures.

Commenting upon his approach to painting problems, he says:

"The birth of an idea is only the beginning of a lengthy period of intense searching into all its aspects. If it survives the test of time and various analyses from the standpoint of space and construction, then I am ready to consider different images of the idea. If it passes this test, as well, the positive medium of paper or canvas is indicated.

"My first step is generally a drawing in black and white, which may best be described as 'notes on the vision' and which is decipherable only by the professional painter. If the idea involves figures, I prepare three or four composition sketches, then I have the models pose substantially in the positions visualized. Whenever possible, I prefer not to use professional models because I find that after a series of studio, commercial, or illustrative poses they often lose the simplicity of ordinary human movement. While it is diffi-

This 9 x 12 wash drawing, in black and sepia, was De Erdely's first graphic study for the picture, "Day's End." He calls these first sketches his "notes on the vision."

This is one of three or four compositional sketches (about 10 x 15) which developed from his original concept as put down in the first "notes on the vision."

PRELIMINARY STUDIES FOR DE ERDELY'S CANVAS, "DAY'S END"

At this stage De Erdely posed models in substantially the positions visualized in the compositional sketches. This is one of several such 20 x 24 studies in black and sepia.

In this step De Erdely has resolved his composition into a geometric pattern as a means of checking the abstract compositional basis of his picture.

De Erdely next prepares a large black-and-white composition, then a color sketch in tempera or pastel. On the canvas itself his first step is to lay-out the geometric construction (see Step 4), then lightly block-in the figures with charcoal.

DAY'S END   OIL   70 x 55

SUMMER SLEEP   OIL   40 x 50

NIGHT   OIL   52 x 42

cult to begin working with an inexperienced model whose shyness and inability to understand the situation have a tendency to inhibit the painter, once the nonprofessional's reserve has been broken down, the painter is rewarded by the model's richer analysis and fuller cooperation. After drawing from the model, I prepare a large black-and-white composition, as well as a color sketch in tempera or pastel, or possibly a combination of both mediums.

"If the original conception was too far-fetched or if imagination has outdistanced knowledge and creative capacity, the exaggeration or shortcoming becomes painfully evident at this stage. During these preliminary stages the conception of the picture has been essentially dualistic, what was conceived as a dramatic vision having been simultaneously abstracted through thought. The final image and the inner structure are developing at the same time.

"After the color sketch has been completed, I turn to the canvas. I suppose it is one of my peculiarities that I must stretch the canvas myself. I prefer a medium-fine weave, which I rub down with sandpaper and treat with oil and turpentine.

"My first step in the construction of the painting is the geometric division of the canvas. Once this is done,

THE FISH MARKET   OIL   40 x 50

I am ready to block my figures lightly into the geometric divisions in charcoal. At this point, the original studies often require alteration in the interest of the final composition, for the reason that a model's attitude may have proved too rigid. The charcoal lines blocking-in the figures are then rubbed off the canvas. But, since the canvas has previously been treated with oil, fine outlines of the figures are still visible. At this and every other stage the canvas must be clean, a personal rule to which I never make any exception. Using a very fine brush, I paint over the faint charcoal lines with burnt umber—afterwards indicating with a heavier brush the distribution of light and dark areas. This clears up the linear and spatial problems.

"When I begin to paint, I find that all my preliminary graphic studies must be forgotten. They have served their purpose of liberating my brush from problems of line and space, thereby giving it the fullest measure of freedom. I build my color scheme up by using the system of the conflict of warm and cold colors, blended of course with light. In the event that I reach a point where my conception appears to be wanting, I recall the model and work with him for a few hours, continuing to paint even after he has left in order to synchronize form and color in the painting, which a shaft of reality sometimes throws out of key.

"To use an expression common to the painting profession, when I have completely 'killed' my idea, the painting is finished.

"As a rule I do not use more than one model at a time, nor do I employ photographs, posed or otherwise. Here, however, I want to digress in order to give the photographer his due. While we painters have taught him how to compose and how to deal with light and shadow, he in turn, especially the motion picture cameraman, has taught us how to see from hitherto unknown or unexplored angles.

"To pass from the technical to the spiritual, in my student years at the Royal Academy of Art at Budapest after World War I, Rembrandt's work was a powerful influence. This was a natural result of the struggles experienced by my generation during the turbulent period, which inclined us toward a sombre fantasy and a preoccupation with the drama of humanity. My devotion to Rembrandt at that time sprang more from reverence for his technical achievements than from any thorough comprehension of his genius. Other strong early influences were Daumier and Goya, who may be said to belong to the same 'family' of painters as Rembrandt. After completing my studies in Budapest, I was led by some adolescent intuition to Goya's work in the Prado—he was closer to me in point of time and more easily digestible than Rembrandt. During my years in Madrid I visited the Museum almost daily, concentrating on the work of Goya, Ribera, Zurbarán, and Velazquez to the complete exclusion of El Greco, Titian, and Tintoretto, despite the fact that the latter are very well represented in the Prado. It was only when I revisited Madrid, years later, that I realized the magnitude of my sin of omission, particularly in the case of El Greco, and I have not forgiven myself to this day.

"While I lived and worked in Paris, Daumier, Delacroix, and Poussin were dominant influences. When I moved to Belgium, I could not escape the spell of Bosch and Brueghel, but their influence for the most part affected my conception of painting rather than my technique. After moving to The Netherlands, in 1931, I had a splendid opportunity to renew my acquaintance with the work of Rembrandt, my youthful ideal. But by that time I had reached a state of maturity and I was able to laugh at my early attempts to imitate his technique, for Rembrandt's full genius was now very apparent to me and no less apparent was the folly of attempting to reach the heights which he had scaled.

"When World War I broke out, I was at the impressionable age of ten. Ever since that holocaust, the history of much of the world, particularly Central Europe, has been a series of armed conflicts and social upheavals and dislocations. The great actor in this drama has been the human being. Therefore it is not surprising that man should be a more fascinating subject of study to me than landscape, still life, or ivory tower *l'art pour l'art*."

Francis de Erdely is an artist who has been thoroughly schooled in the ideals and the technique of traditional painting—sound draftsmanship, studied composition, persuasive surfaces, color harmony.

One is impressed by the spiritual quality of his work no less than by its technical aspects. We cannot escape the conclusion that the people who inhabit De Erdely's canvases are considerably more than pictorial props in esthetic essays; they are human beings in whom, as representatives of classes and conditions, the artist has deep interest.

De Erdely was born in Budapest, Hungary, in 1904. He is a graduate of the Royal Academy of Art of Budapest. He also studied at the Academy San Fernando in Madrid, the Sorbonne in Paris, and in the Louvre. His pugilistic experience, already noted, financed his studies for several years in Spain.

De Erdely at this writing is a Professor of Painting at the University of Southern California and a member of the faculty of the Jepson Art Institute of Los Angeles.

His work is in the permanent collections of the museums of Madrid, Barcelona, Amsterdam, The Hague, Brussels, Antwerp, Ghent, Mons, Bratislava, Algiers, Jeu de Paume, Detroit Institute of Arts, M. H. De Young Memorial Museum of San Francisco, Los Angeles County Museum, Pasadena Art Institute, Denver Art Museum, and the National Gallery of Victoria in Melbourne, Australia.

Although his art is seen most frequently in exhibitions in the American West, it hangs also in national offerings in such leading institutions as the Corcoran Gallery in Washington, D. C., the Pennsylvania Academy of the Fine Arts, Cleveland Museum of Art, Virginia Museum of Art, Grand Rapids Art Museum, John Herron Art Institute of Indianapolis and the Art Institute of Chicago. He was represented in the Pepsi-Cola "Paintings of the Year" exhibitions in 1946, 1947 and 1948, and in the same years in the Carnegie Institute's series of "Painting in the United States."

Grigory Gluckmann

Grigory Gluckman painting the canvas "Etude"

DRESSING ROOM   OIL   17 x 20

Grigory Gluckmann
a contemporary "old master"

GRIGORY GLUCKMANN, who has lived and worked in America since 1940, spent the earlier years of his career in Paris. He's an internationally known painter, having won prizes and honors on both sides of the Atlantic. His canvases are owned by the Luxembourg Museum and the Petit Palais Museum of Paris, the Museum of the City of Havre, France, the Art Institute of Chicago, the Fine Arts Society of San Diego, the Encyclopaedia Britannica and other noted collections. The canvas *Confidences,* reproduced here in color, was invited to Carnegie's 1947 Annual Exhibition in Pittsburgh.

Although Gluckmann paints occasional landscapes, he is definitely a figure painter. Many of his canvases are single figure subjects, but his compositions of several figures are among his most interesting productions. In these the figures are skillfully arranged and the pictures are constructed upon well-conceived abstract foundations.

Of some painters it can be said that they are good draftsmen who paint well; others merit the observation that they are good painters who are competent draftsmen. Gluckmann belongs in the latter category. He is essentially a painter; from the first brush mark on his canvas to the picture's completion his approach is through tonality and color. He begins at once to brush-in masses of color without any preliminary line drawing. Even in the first hours of painting he insists upon capturing the subtle aspects of the subject. This is quite evident in the photographic record of his painting of *Etude,* which is the result of about ninety hours of direct painting from the model, in thirty three-hour sittings. The figure in *Etude* is so similar to one in *Confidences* that its color can be envisioned when studying the color plate.

Gluckmann's color is invariably rich and muted; it is always tonal, always noted for the currently unfashionable characteristic of "quality"; it is often designated "old mastery."

Gluckmann's brush work is meticulous; he works exclusively with sable brushes. These contribute to the "caress" which he so appreciatively imparts to flesh tones and textures. But the artist's affection for these tonal and color "perfections" seems never to distract him from the tectonic qualities of the canvas. Largeness of conception and unity of design are, in fact, aspects of his work that are often emphasized by critics.

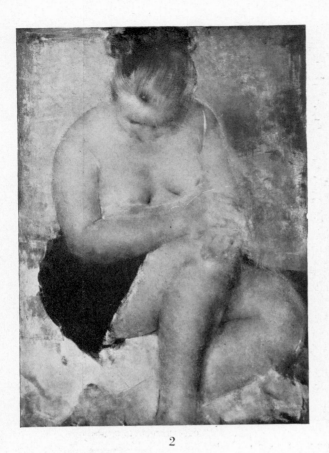

3

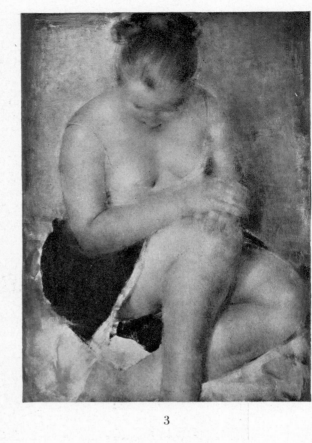

2

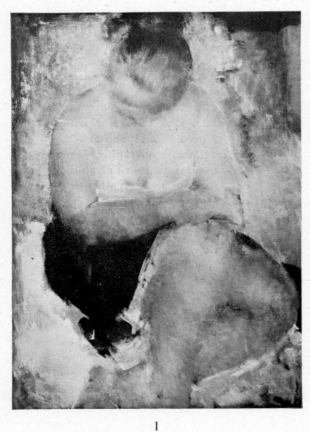

1

STEPS IN THE

DEVELOPMENT OF

"ETUDE"

BY GRIGORY GLUCKMANN

The painting of "Etude," reproduced in halftone on the opposite page, extended over a period of five weeks. During that time there were thirty separate three-hour poses by the model.

The three photographs of the canvas in progress were spaced at such intervals as seemed best to show its development. Note that even in the first stage, photographed after the first sitting, Gluckmann has captured much of the spirit and even subtlety of the finished picture.

There was no preliminary drawing on the canvas, the artist beginning at once to work in mass and color. The drawing and the form emerge as the picture progresses.

Gluckmann paints directly, does not practice underpainting or underglazing. He works entirely with sable brushes.

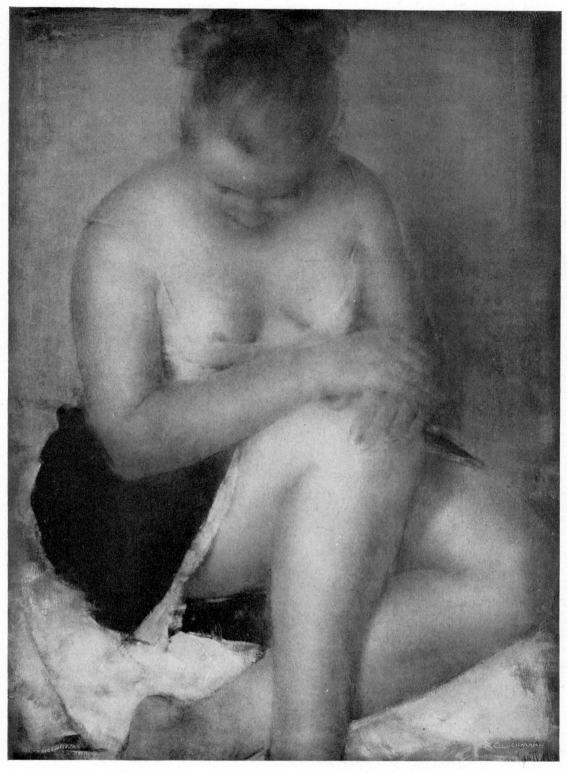

ETUDE   OIL   28 x 21

This painting was executed on a three-quarter-inch plywood panel. It is similar in color to one of the figures in "Confidences." (See color reproduction.)

NUDE   WATERCOLOR

Gluckmann's competence as a craftsman is in the tradition of good painting—as it persisted up to recent times, when the impulse to shock began to supersede the ideal of power through restraint and control—through the employment of all those artifices that make every square inch of the canvas contribute its note to the harmony of a skillfully orchestrated color symphony. That is something of a rarity today, and with the passing years fewer still remain who have the power to delight us with their craftsmanship.

Looking at a Gluckmann canvas, something which Thomas Bodkin wrote about Chardin in his book, *The Approach to Painting,* comes to mind:

"Chardin handled paint as though he loved it for its own sake. We feel that each touch of the brush is a lingering caress. He does not slap on or polish his pigment. He wipes it gently, ruffles it, thickens it into a curd of impasto, he thins it into a vale of lucid glaze;

he nurses it with brushes, palette knife or thumb until it lies softly and lightly, a temptation to our fingertips, a delight to our eyes, a prime example of all that painters mean when they speak of 'quality' of color."

This is not quoted to imply that Gluckmann's methods are those of Chardin. Bodkin's words, however, are quite expressive of what must be Gluckmann's attitude toward his art. At any rate, the net result of his procedure, like that of Chardin, is indeed a "temptation to our fingertips, a delight to our eyes."

Gluckmann's reputation rests primarily upon his oils, but when he essays a watercolor the picture usually turns out to be a good Gluckmann, even a prize-winning performance.

Grigory Gluckmann at 51 is at the summit of a very successful and satisfying career; he paints what he wants to paint, and enough people crave his product to keep him busy. What more can a painter desire?

Julian Levi

ABANDONED POWERHOUSE OIL 22 x 28

Julian Levi

painter with a melancholy brush

JULIAN LEVI in discussing his approach to painting has quoted Georges Rouault, one of his graphic heroes, who said about his own work, "In truth I have painted by opening my eyes day and night on the perceptible world and also by closing them from time to time that I might better see the vision blossom and submit itself to orderly arrangement."

Of course there is nothing very profound about this; it might have been written by almost any imaginative painter. It is merely another way of saying that what sets one artist above the unexciting average and makes his art something more than a fleeting pleasantry is the quality of an inner vision that takes the facts of natural appearance, reshapes them, colors them and employs them as symbols in a personal commentary upon life.

The "quality" of the inner vision, while it does not wholly deny analysis, is as mysterious as personality itself. It is, in fact, personality made articulate. There are the imponderables of heredity and the emotional trends, interests and behavior tendencies engendered in formative years. No amount of adult education and influence will greatly alter the ego thus created, although they can and do give direction for its expansion.

Can we not then assume that the art of Julian Levi is noteworthy, not because the artist happened to be born at just the right time to come under the influence of modern art but because what he is saying in his pictures represents the reactions of an extremely sensitive nature to the experiences of an entire lifetime. It is, of course, impossible to envision what his canvases would have looked like had he come upon the scene fifty years earlier and known only the language of traditional painting. But granted his importance today, it is logical that he would have distinguished himself in any era.

As a matter of fact, Levi in his youth chose the language of the moderns. His art education began in Philadelphia at the Pennsylvania Academy of the Fine Arts where he found himself drawn to the rebellious moderns Arthur Carles and Henry McCarter, who were teaching at the Academy. A Cresson Travelling Scholarship in 1920 took him abroad for study. After a few months in Italy, where he adopted Massacio as one of his heroes, he went to Paris. During the next four years he was a disciple of the French moderns, with some of whom he became intimate. "Pascin," he says, "was a true friend who guided me into a profound appreciation of draftsmanship. He insisted on my sketching indiscriminately wherever I happened to be."

As to Picasso, Leger and the abstractionists, these he declares, "led to experimentation in that direction which served as invaluable discipline in the architecture of painting."

It is a tribute to Levi that having sat at the feet of these masters he has assimilated those influences that he found useful to his purpose and developed his own personal language, a language that does not recognizably reflect any one of them. He has, in consequence, escaped the modern academy and has justly won acclaim as a creative modern.

As to the quality of his inner vision, that is consistently communicated in all his canvases, which are the product of much brooding and experimentation. He produces less than a dozen paintings a year. His is an introspective, a contemplative art. It cannot be accomplished, he declares, "by pictorial rhetoric or the manipulation of seductive paint surfaces. Nor is a good picture concocted out of theatrical props, beautiful subjects, or memories of other paintings. All these might astound but they will never communicate the emotional content or exaltation of life."

There is no definition of the "beautiful." But Julian Levi's landscapes of the ocean's shore are not the pretty scenes that pleasure seekers record on kodachrome. The objects that catch his eye and stir his imagination are blackened skeletons of half-buried hulks, rotting piles, dilapidated shacks, flotsam and jetsam—mournful mementoes of man's defeated hopes, evidence of brief victories turned to routs in an unequal battle with time and the elements. His impressions of beach and dunes are painted with a melancholy brush. He is obsessed with the loneliness of deserted sands, gray under leaden skies and littered with wreckage cast up by the sea or by a battered and rusty ship's boiler tossed on the rocks by storms. Whenever man intrudes upon a Levi canvas his presence serves to enhance the loneliness of the scene. And usually the human presence is without sentiment or deep meaning. An exception is *The Widow* (see color plate) wherein the sorrowing woman

As he always does, Levi made innumerable sketches and studies for this canvas, which he painted in 1945. The lower left halftone is reproduced from a 9 x 12 ink-and-sepia study. The lower right one is a color study made with ordinary wax crayons. Note the scraping with a sharp point. The pencil study, directly below, is from a live model.

LOBSTERMAN   OIL   27 x 19

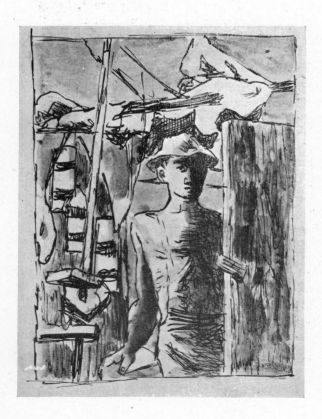

CAPE COD MORNING OIL

becomes the central object of interest. Far from being a mere accessory she is actually the incentive for the picture, having her origin in the painter's sympathy for a bereaved woman of his acquaintance. The canvas is the result of continuous pondering throughout a long period of time, from which nearly fifty studies in various mediums remain.

If, as some contend, that canvas is a bit sentimental, *Abandoned Powerhouse* evidences the artist's skill in achieving an even more nostalgic mood without recourse to theatrical means. But whatever the means, Levi is sure to invoke a fragrant melancholy mood in all his pictures. That, so far as content is concerned, is his inner vision. We see it even in his figure subjects; in the wistful face and hesitating attitude of the *Lobsterman,* and in the portrait of Suba, whose physiognomy is strikingly similar to the lobsterman's.

Levi admits that his interest in people is secondary. In his figure and portrait subjects he is not so unquestionably Levi as in his landscapes. He says he seldom finds his models among people of superlative beauty or symmetry, is fascinated by "brats" of eight or nine. His wife, he confides, "submits graciously to assaults I make on her beauty."

Levi deprecates the lure of "seductive paint surfaces." And his canvases, truly enough, are not espe-

SUBA, A PORTRAIT OIL 29 x 21

WELLFLEET HARBOR 1941 OIL

cially notable for paint quality. They do not suggest that Levi "loves paint for its own sake." But he knows how to paint and his technical equipment is wholly adequate. His color is subtle and gray as befits his mood and he is most successful when he stays within the range of sombre hues.

Levi does a great deal of preliminary work for every canvas he paints. Through innumerable sketches and studies the picture's concept is gradually crystalized and its details developed in drawings. When he begins to paint he knows exactly what he expects the picture to look like; accidents play an almost negligible part. Once he starts a painting he keeps at work on it until it is finished, although he may have several pictures going at the same time.

Since early boyhood when summers found him at Hyannis, Massachusetts, Julian Levi has spent as much time as possible at the seashore. As a lad he sought the company of sailors and fishermen. One of his father's employees who was a tobacco broker had been a sailor. From him Julian learned the lore of ships and the sea. He made ship models and later he sailed an 11-foot dinghy in Barnegat Bay, New Jersey. To his studio in New York he has brought a quantity of fishermen's gear to supply at least a whiff of the atmosphere so essential to his creative experiences.

Levi's work is to be seen in the permanent collections of over fifteen leading American museums. It enjoys the somewhat unique distinction of a high rating in both modern and traditional circles. It succeeds, in an unusual degree, to reach the goal envisioned by Levi when he said, "I try to remember that painting at its best is a form of communication, that it is constantly reaching out to find response from an ideal and sympathetic audience." This, of course, is quite a different ambition from the desire for communication with the largest possible audience, the kind of audience that votes the popular prize. Levi's pictures are for those who have something themselves to give in exchange for the pleasures the painter reserves for the sympathetic seeker.

Born in New York in 1900, Levi held his first one-man exhibition in 1933 at the Crillon Galleries in Philadelphia, following it in 1940, 1942 and 1944 by similar shows in New York's Downtown Gallery.

Among the awards he has received are two from the Art Institute of Chicago: the Kohnstamm Prize (1942) and Norman Wait Harris Medal (1943); a prize from Pepsi-Cola's "Paintings of the Year" (1945); the Obrig Prize of the National Academy of Design (1945), and, in 1948, a Purchase Award from the University of Illinois.

In addition to representation in the permanent collections of many of the country's leading museums and galleries, his paintings may be found in the University of Arizona, University of Georgia, in the New Trier Township High School of Winnetka, Illinois, and in the Encyclopaedia Britannica Collection. He now teaches in New York at the Art Students League and at the New School.

Donald Mattison

LOW TIDE   OIL   36 x 42

Donald Mattison
painter of a joyous world

DONALD MATTISON paints for a living world, and he paints what that world can understand and enjoy—its own life. What is more, he chooses to paint subjects that record life's pleasanter moments—children gazing into candy-shop windows, boys playing at soldier, youngsters flying kites, girls out for a lark on an excursion steamer.

Mattison appears to find plenty of excitement in the normal exuberance of youth. Not that warm and wholesome themes have anything to do with the quality of his art; none the less they are a refreshing contrast to much current painting which reflects the turbulence of our present-day world. Such occasional reminders as Mattison gives us of the eternal promise of youth go far to restore our faith in the ultimate victory of truth and beauty.

Mattison, director of John Herron Art School, Indianapolis, Indiana, and a product of the Yale Art School and the American Academy in Rome (Prix de Rome, 1928), remains true to those influences and the traditional concepts of painting that antedate the experiments of the ultramoderns. These concepts are undoubtedly best suited to the nature of his interests and the quality of his vision.

Mattison is a deliberate, studious worker with an analytical approach. Before starting his final painting he develops his design quite completely in a series of experiments like those shown here. Thus, when beginning to paint he knows just what he is going to do. This is not to say that the accidental is wholly lacking in the progress of the picture, but it certainly is reduced to a minimum.

"Lucky is the painter," says Mattison, "who is able to rush to his canvas and with a few strokes of the brush put down quickly a complete and meaningful picture. For me, after making a rapid sketch on any old scrap of paper that happens to be in my pocket at the moment, the first, and one of the most important, steps in the development of the canvas is an analysis of the idea and a definition of the basic emotion. I have found that a word definition is most helpful in clarifying the problem.

"In working from such a basic and abstract beginning as a single word which expresses the main theme [*Concert, Goodby, Return, Carnival* and *Excursion* are among Mattison's one-word titles], I find it possible to come closer to the universal than by a literal acceptance of a first spontaneous sketch. Whatever qualities of imagination, expression, or nostalgia may be felt in the picture *Parade,* for example, were made more nearly possible in the final canvas by employing this method of idea analysis first." (See color plate.)

Asked to explain the part this method of idea analysis played in the creation of *Parade,* Mattison said:

"*Parade* seems to be a simple enough picture and the meaning is self-evident. Although it was inspired by the exhilaration experienced at the conclusion of the war, and the picture was my way of expressing the emotion of precisely that moment, perhaps it also is a picture of all the parades I had ever seen. I expect that our responses to experiences are often more complicatd than we immediately suppose, and things remembered stir around in the painter's mind for a long time before they are awakened and fired by some contemporary

SECOND STUDY

Greater control of definite forms and their relationship was attempted here. Spaces have been made more compact and the figures have become larger in relation to the window.

THIRD STUDY

In this final design-cartoon depth has been better realized and the strong oblique movement of the figures to the left gives more dynamic contrast to the swirling lines.

FIRST STUDY FOR "PARADE"
(See color reproduction)

This first sketch, in Wolff pencil on bond paper, shows the general action and lighting, the contrast of straight and curved lines, and the box-like framework surrounding the swirling figures that complement each other. The spirit of the subject is spontaneously indicated.

stimulus finally to become a picture. The nostalgia of remembered events gives meaning somehow to the present. The war brought back the parade feeling and added its own emotion.

"I don't know why I chose three young girls for the picture rather than three old girls or three old boys. Perhaps it was because in my recollection of the people who lean from windows to see parades they were always young girls. At any rate, I had them in mind from the start and followed that impulse through.

"Of all the fascinating and decorative material offered the painter in a parade, the event itself seemed to interest me least. Most poignantly of all, I remembered the spectators, how they looked and acted and responded; for in them was my chief interest—human emotion. Pictorial material was provided by people crowded into a window hardly large enough to hold all of the swirling arms and active bodies, turning heads, and colorful and exciting shapes which I could employ in the expression of my theme."

It is axiomatic that the painter must feel a strong emotional response to his subject in beginning a canvas, but Mattison puts a lot of emphasis upon the conscious effort that is required to understand the quality of that emotion. His ideas, bound up as they are with things remembered, make especially important the word analysis, and it is the first of many problems of technique. Says Mattison:

"I use composition to function in the interests of the theme. The lines, shapes, colors and values not only must be interesting in themselves—they must form combinations for the purpose of expression. In working out a canvas, I like to think of the finished picture as an ideal blend of means and meaning, each inseparable from the other. Certainly this notion is not new, and each artist creates his own style in this way. For some artists this results in an abstract style. In *Parade* I wanted the look of reality.

"From the beginning, the sketches progressed from the back-of-an-envelope stage to the point where the design expressed the exact feeling as first conceived

COLOR STUDY

This pastel study is one of several color sketches done at intervals, between pencil studies, for design. The scheme of color was based upon the flag. The three notes of red, white and blue were varied in intensity and quality throughout the design with one or two contrasting notes of yellow and green. The large areas were modified and the small ones intensified for balance and contrast. Movement was achieved by placing similar color spots so that they followed one after another in the path of the linear scheme and by contrasting the left and right extremes of the canvas with warm and cool notes. Movement in depth was achieved by the use of warm, bright colors in the foreground, cooler and grayer colors toward the back.

and defined. Excitement and exhilaration necessarily implied considerable movement in the composition. The lines had to have that quality; the colors, shapes and values were to be given contrasts that were active to induce the holiday spirit of the theme. I was especially concerned that with each step of the designing and execution of *Parade* the feeling of *life* should be emphasized.

"Having given form to my theme through countless composition and color sketches, it was possible to paint from the model in the beginning without fear of falling into a too literal transcription from nature. I built a small stage in my studio to resemble, in a rough way, the window setting of the picture, and posed the models in it. This proved to be worth while because the lighting from nature gave me the key to the effect of the whole canvas.

"Thus it was that the three models, posed at different times, were brought into one picture in a unified way. They were used only to start the first work on the canvas, following which the painting was finished independently of the models."

Mattison likes to start the actual painting on the canvas with a thin and light-toned wash of color over the various areas, as indicated by the color study. This starts the canvas as a whole with an over-all envelop-

FIGURE STUDY

Mattison worked directly from a model while laying-in each figure on the canvas. Figure studies such as this, done later from memory of the model, guided his selection of forms, and use of lighting, figure action and character in developing the canvas.

ANALYSIS OF MOVEMENT
Curves and straight lines move from the upright, at the far right, to the left —emphasizing action. Oblique lines, representing the direction of the trunks of the figures, and curves, indicating the flying arms, convey excitement.

ANALYSIS OF PATTERN
Values were designed to follow the movement from right to left, revealing shapes that emphasize the whirl of excitement, creating a dramatic contrast of light and dark areas, suggesting the movement of planes from front to back, and indicating modeling and direction of lighting.

ANALYSIS OF LINE
Comparison with the final painting (see color plate) will reveal the relationship between the small and large shapes. These follow the general spirit of the movement and grow out of the large design, and, by linear repetition, become symphonically expressive of the theme of excitement.

CONCERT   OIL   36 x 42

ment in its first stage. This first color often appears through the direct painting which follows, and so is useful as the forms are gradually painted-in and the values become richer and the details are finally and fully realized. He tries to keep all parts of the picture consistent in each stage of the painting. Since the forms are built up gradually, the bolder contrasts, strongest definitions and thickest paint are put on toward the last. A kind of pervading luminosity results, with opaque and transparent passages complementing each other. He avoids sable brushes; with them he can never get the effects that he wants. Bristle brushes are quite suitable for his purpose. When a bit of painting gets out of hand, he scrapes that area and starts afresh.

Says Mattison, "I have developed these technical means as best suited to the expression of the ideas that interest me most. The ideas, it so happens, are on the affirmative side of existence, and to me are all-important. Since we can't avoid some debt to others, I suppose that what counts is the bit that one adds to the tradition in which he works. The tradition to which one elects to belong seems rather unimportant in itself. What the artist can give of his own vision becomes his paramount and final concern."

Donald Mattison was born in Beloit, Wisconsin, in 1905, and lived there until his family moved to North Carolina in 1920. In 1928 he was graduated from the Yale School of Fine Arts, where he studied under Eugene Savage. The Prix de Rome award, won upon graduation, took him abroad for three years in the American Academy in Rome. Upon his return, he taught for a few years at Columbia University and at New York University. Since 1933, Mattison has been director of John Herron Art School. He says, "I am happy to be one of those art school directors who consider themselves first of all professional painters, and I apportion my time between the two occupations with this in mind. I find this works toward the best interests of school and painter.

"As a teacher," he observes, "it is a satisfaction to me that my students have been featured in such publications as *Life* and *Time* magazines, that their work is accepted for regional and national exhibitions, and that they are receiving prizes and having their work purchased by important museums. They also hold positions in outstanding university art departments and in art schools throughout the country."

Mattison himself is a prize winner. In 1947 he won a $500 third prize in the L. S. Ayres & Co. 75th Anniversary Exhibition of Indiana Artists for his *Christmas at Orchard;* in 1948 the Robertine Daniels Prize in the Indiana Artists Club Annual for *Low Tide;* the Indiana Artists Club Prize in that body's 1949 Annual for *Conversation,* and honorable mention the same year in the Annual National Exhibition of the Delgado Museum, New Orleans, for his *Evening.*

In addition to his teaching and portrait painting, Mattison has served on the Board of Control in the Midwestern College Art Conference, as well as on various juries for exhibitions in the Middle West.

Henry Mattson

Henry Mattson

an original and poetic painter

NO GREATER FORTUNE could come to a painting student than to know Henry Mattson. I do not say "study painting" with him. No, do not go to him with palette and brushes in hand: a thousand good painters can better teach how to organize a picture, set a palette and master technical problems of pigment and medium. One would no more expect Mattson to teach these things than to ask Einstein for instruction in elementary physics. Go to Mattson eager for the spirit, not the substance; seeking a clue to those imponderables that differentiate art from mere good painting.

We must approach this artist from the standpoint of emotional content, not of technical performance. Unlike many painters whose canvases bespeak an artist's delight in sheer craftsmanship—pigments, brush work, and elegance of manner—Mattson sacrifices surface interest and obvious charm in order to express that which is deeply felt rather than seen. He is concerned with mood, not melody. This is not to say that his painting lacks technical distinction, or that his craftsmanship is in any way inferior to his art, but he is not interested in craftsmanship as such. His studio equipment and his method of work attest to that. Two brushes only, one an ordinary house-painter's brush, serve for the painting of all his canvases. His palette, a porcelain-topped table, resembles a no-man's land of mingled colors. This, in contrast to the profusion of professional equipment and meticulous organization seen in the studios of most painters.

Mattson is a poetic and original painter. He belongs to no school, nor can we trace the influence of other painters upon his work. If he reminds us of any artist who has gone before, it is that American old master, Albert P. Ryder, who was also a dreamer and poet. Not that their work has any superficial likeness; the similarity is in type of mind and in conception of the creative function of art. Ryder dwelt in an imaginary world illumined by a "light that never was on land or sea." So does Mattson.

Such painters do not readily win popular acclaim. As Daniel Gregory Mason has said, "Art of any profundity can be appreciated only slowly, gradually, in leisurely contemplation." In this connection, too, Frank Jewett Mather, Jr., once remarked, in effect—while discussing forgeries of masterpieces—that a really great work of art reserves its charms only for the patient seeker after beauty; that the experts are skeptical when, too readily, they fall in love with a work of art upon first sight of it.

Henry Mattson was born in Sweden in 1887. When he was eighteen he emigrated to America, with thirteen dollars in his pocket, and got a job in a machine shop in Worcester, Massachusetts. He had no thought of becoming an artist, though from his boyhood he had loved pictures and had availed himself of every opportunity for seeing them. In Worcester he attended art exhibitions on Saturdays and Sundays; and made frequent trips to nearby Boston for the same purpose while his fellows were at ball games.

Walking downtown one Saturday night in 1912, he was attracted by a window display in an artists' supply store. The object that caught his eye was a mahogany paint box outfitted with the usual array of paints and brushes. "It looked so damn good, I went in and bought it," said Mattson, recalling that historic incident. "The price was something over eight dollars." He still has that paint box although he has not used it for twenty years. It was the spark that ignited a smouldering, though, until then, unrecognized desire to create pictures instead of merely to enjoy them.

Thus, Henry Mattson began to paint. He worked by himself, wholly without instruction except for a short period when he drew from the cast in the night classes of the Worcester Museum. As grotesque an "art" education as could be conjured up for a man like Mattson who never could submit to the discipline of drawing, who always has conceived in terms of brush and color.

His desire to become a professional painter grew and he decided to return to Sweden to study there under a master of considerable repute. Always frugal, Mattson had saved nine hundred dollars for this adventure in art. Back home, he presented himself to his prospective mentor and hopefully displayed his paintings for criticism. The master was unimpressed, so much so that he even refused Mattson admission to his studio, declaring that he had declined to accept students who were infinitely more talented. That was a cruel blow, but it did not weaken the young man's determination to become a painter. Henry is, as Mrs. Mattson confides, "awfully stubborn." The rebuff merely drove him back to America and to Chicago, where he rented a studio and devoted himself exclusively to painting as long as his money held out. Then he got a job as machinist—becoming shop foreman—and from 1913 to 1916 he practiced his trade and spent every spare hour with his paint box.

Courtesy the Carnegie Institute

BLACK REEF OIL

SELF-PORTRAIT OIL

Mattson has painted more than a dozen self-portraits. Many of them are in public and private collections.

The urge to paint finally became so compelling, that he decided, come what may, he would leave the machine shop for good and embark upon a painter's career. He had heard about Woodstock, New York, the home of many famous artists, and that, as he says, "he could have contact with the world of art and starve much more slowly and comfortably than in the city." He did not starve, though he did endure many years of such struggle as have to be borne by so many artists in the early years of their careers. Upon his arrival in Woodstock he entered John Carlson's painting class, but he stuck it out for only three months. He had to go his own way, alone; his creative urge was so strong that he could not abide the discipline of technical instruction. He had to develop wholly from the inside out.

Thus Mattson went his own way, pioneering in the realm of his individual genius, self-taught and uninfluenced by the work of his fellow artists, though warm in their companionship and esteem. He sold a picture now and then, earned a little money teaching manual training in a Woodstock private school, managed to get along somehow. In 1924, he married Daphne Sawyer Grimm.

Recognition came slowly. His pictures began to win prizes, to be purchased by museums and collectors.

Success has not changed Henry Mattson. Accustomed to frugality and by nature preferring the simple life, he is today content with the scantiest material possessions. "Henry isn't interested in things," his wife explains. "He would have barely enough furniture in the house for comfort if he had his way."

The Mattson home in Woodstock is indeed a modest abode. It is an ancient structure that originally housed two village stores, and in the rear a blacksmith shop which has been converted into a living room. The garret serves as a studio. Its roof has been raised somewhat and a skylight built into its north slope. The old brick chimney in the center of the house divides the room into studio and garret, the dark end appearing to be a typical attic catchall. Mrs. Mattson warned me that, "You'll find the studio is a mess; that's the way Henry likes it." She called my attention also to his scrambled palette and disorderly table with tubes of paint thrown carelessly about. She picked up one tube after another and screwed on their tops. "See how careless Henry is with these expensive paints. He's so economical in every way except with his painting."

It is Mattson's custom to paint in the late afternoon and evening. That is consistent with the mood of his pictures and his own brooding nature. The sun seldom shines in his pictures, which are usually painted in an eerie and foreboding light and are infused with an epic kind of loneliness. No one ever sees Mattson painting in the fields and lanes of Woodstock. Indeed, he never paints from nature or from models. No canvases of his are replicas of anything seen with the physical eye. For that reason many of them have a supernatural quality not readily appreciated by the literal-minded. Mattson does not even paint from memory, that is, from conscious memory. A mood, an aspect, or detail of nature may sink into his subconscious mind and bob up later to be incorporated in a painting, but no matter how much he may be impressed by a scene or a passing mood of nature he never tries to carry the impression back to his studio, to put it on canvas.

Mattson's pictures are absolutely unpremeditated. When he stands before a fresh canvas and begins to paint, he seldom knows nor does he try to plan the picture that will finally evolve. He relies upon "ideas that

THE LIFE BOAT OIL

"A sailor doesn't think of the beauty of the ocean," says Mattson. "To him it is a fundamental condition of his daily life and it is his diverse experience with the sea rather than esthetic appearance that impresses him. In my pictures I try to express such fundamental reactions to this terrifying natural element."

Rehn Galleries

come from nowhere." These finally lead him in a direction which he consciously pursues, thus developing the theme and rounding it out as his sense of order and organization dictates. His compositional sense is purely intuitive as he has no theories of color or picture structure. He is not analytical. He cannot explain why he does this or that in his canvas, except that he felt it should be that way.

All Mattson starts with is an urge to paint. He may begin with a tree and end with a painting of the sea. Mrs. Mattson declares she is shocked to note, upon looking into his studio from time to time, that the subject matter of a canvas, seen an hour previously, has been substituted by something entirely different. An astonishing example of this radical change of purpose is the painting of the sleeping cat. This canvas started as a mountain, snow clad and patterned with patches of tawny color where the snow had melted. "As I was painting this," said Mattson, "a cat jumped up on the chair nearby. I noticed that her color was exactly like that of the tawny patches on the mountain and I had an impulse to paint the cat instead of the

NIGHT WITCHERY OIL

Mattson's brush is inspired by nature's most awesome aspects. He is concerned with mood rather than melody.

Rehn Galleries
Juley Photo

MATTSON'S PALETTE

An enamel-topped table is a no-man's land of scrambled colors.

mountain. So I did." At another time he started to paint a nude and before long discovered he had a landscape on his canvas.

Mattson's approach to painting is as simple as that. "I haven't any ideas at all," he will tell you. "I just paint what comes to me at the time. I am not interested in painting what everyone sees in nature, but of my own experiences with nature."

Mattson paints the ocean more than anything else. He has crossed the Atlantic nine times and has summered in Rockport on the Massachusetts coast. But he has never made on-the-spot studies of the sea. Instead, he goes back to his Woodstock studio and paints his impressions in leisurely contemplation. In explaining his approach to these canvases he says, "I paint the sea because I love it and fear it too. I think about it constantly, not so much what it looks like at any particular time but I think about its elemental aspect, its weight, its awesome depth, the powerful action of its waters. A sailor doesn't think of the beauty of the ocean. To him it is a fundamental condition of his daily life and it is his diverse experiences with the sea rather than esthetic appearances that impress him.

In my pictures I try to express such fundamental, even primitive, reactions to this rather terrifying natural element." The artist feels something of this same psychological reaction to great rock masses and waterfalls, which are frequent subjects of his canvases.

I have explained that Mattson paints neither from nature nor models. An exception must be made, of course, in referring to his self-portraits, of which he has—astonishingly enough—painted a dozen or more. But even in these self-portraits he has not allowed himself to be held down by the reality of his subject. Speaking of his method in these portraits, he said, "I used a mirror the first day or so to sketch in the basic lines and forms and then I forgot all about myself."

Henry Mattson is represented in twenty-two American museums and private collections, including the White House in Washington, D.C., and the Metropolitan and Whitney museums in New York. He has done two murals for the U. S. Post Office in Portland, Maine, and has received many awards, among them the Guggenheim Fellowship, 1935; Norman Wait Harris Prize, the Art Institute of Chicago, 1931; Worcester Art Museum Prize, 1933; the Corcoran Bronze Medal, 1935; Carnegie International third prize, 1935; and first prize for his *Rocks* at the 1942 Corcoran Biennial.

In 1945 Mattson won the Jennie Sesnan Medal at the Pennsylvania Academy of the Fine Arts for *The Life Boat,* here reproduced. A year later his marine, *Atlantic,* claimed the $500 Salmagundi Club Award, and, in 1947, he received an Anonymous Prize of $700 from the National Academy of Design to which he was elected an Associate Member in 1948. In 1950 he was awarded the Beck Medal for the "Best Portrait" in the Annual Exhibition in the Pennsylvania Academy of the Fine Arts.

Mattson's painting tools are a number five artist's bristle brush and a one-inch house painter's brush.

Henry Lee McFee

CROW WITH PEACHES   OIL

Henry Lee McFee
a discussion of his still life painting

HENRY LEE MCFEE, for many years associated with the art colony in Woodstock, New York, is a subtle painter of simple things.

Born April 14, 1886, in St. Louis, of American parentage, he had a year's formal art training at Pittsburgh in 1907, before he went to Woodstock in 1908 to study landscape painting under Birge Harrison, at that time a teacher in the Summer School conducted by the Art Students League of New York.

His work in the beginning was of a quality that indicated he could have become a Grade A academic painter, had not an uncompromisingly independent nature led him away from a repetition of academic formulas into an individual way of working and an accomplishment of his own.

He apprehended early that the creative artist's business is to express nature's life rather than to copy nature's shell of appearance—the two being separate and distinct ideas: one resulting from subjective seeing or mind's sight, the other from objective seeing or eye sight.

He was aided in the direction he had chosen by an absorbing interest and study of the esthetic theories of Cézanne and the postimpressionists. He became interested in cubism, early in his career, and painted cubist pictures for several years. A number of these canvases are significant contributions to that movement in this country.

His direction of research in three-dimensional form began around 1920.

His pictures are lushly painted and rich in harmonious color. The color interprets essential planes quite as much as the drawing does, in order to give objects a "form life" of their own.

"I am interested," McFee says, "in all the things I find about me—in nature, in the look of people, the way they group themselves. I like cities and almost all the things I find in them with which I become completely familiar. But that is only the beginning. It is not until I find something that is really for me, that I begin to think and plan; and later work, to build up my unit of design (my canvas).

"I suppose I am more interested in still life because it does not bother me—it does not have to be given a rest every so often and I don't have to keep up a pretended interest in a human being that is before me. I do not have to gossip as I work.

"I'll admit that sometimes I feel that I should like to do groups of people; but actually when it comes to working, a few simple objects do very well.

"I like to work with objects that are in themselves commonplace: I like the very simple thing, the familiar thing, the ordinary thing; then if God is good and I am good I can make that common thing expressive or beautiful, anything you choose to call it. The bouquet of wild flowers and field grasses in a common pitcher interests me more than perfect peonies in a precious vase, against elegant drapery.

"Some of my pictures," the artist continues, "come from what I call 'set-ups.' Others I find in odd places and I paint them as I find them. For the set-ups, I gather on a studio table things that will make an interesting group to paint. Being careful not to get too much illumination on the table, I adjust the curtains of my north window so as to get exactly the lighting that I want. If there is too much light, not only the table but the entire end of the studio is flooded and I cannot get the contrast that I desire. I arrange and rearrange objects and draperies, always endeavoring to find the organic rhythm that will give me a lead into the endlessly complicated thrusts and pulls of the organization. When I feel that I have the makings, I begin to plan the picture—the unit of design that I hope to make expressive.

"I draw with a light, rather thin, blue-gray oil color. The lines of the drawing are thin and gray, but as I proceed and the lines are moved back and forth to develop volumes and to secure balance, the canvas sometimes takes on a strange look that would not mean much, I am afraid, to an untrained eye. Sometimes at this stage I have to stop and make pencil drawings of part of the group, or of a single object, in order to measure my understanding. This is, for me, the 'architecture' of the canvas. To be sure, it is not yet developed in color, but it gives me a pretty secure feeling of how the canvas will build. This planning I do with great care.

"I am not clever with paint. I plan the canvas well and proceed little by little to build it up."

When McFee says he is not clever with paint he

means, of course, that he does not express his ideas in painting casually. Rather, he struggles with the "architecture" of the canvas. What does he mean by that?

Is it not obvious, as we study his canvases, that he means the abstract elements with which he creates his superb designs? What else can account for the great charm of his pictures? Certainly there is no inherent beauty in the ordinary objects he puts together. But, just as the steel girders of a building are the skeletons of its architecture, the abstract foundation—the design of McFee's picture—is the skeleton of his pictorial architecture.

His architecture, however, is achieved by what he has called "the endlessly complicated thrusts and pulls of organization" rather than the more static balance of engineering construction.

Furthermore, the architecture is not subordinated, in the development of the picture, by undue emphasis upon whatever intrinsic charm the objects might possess—as is so often the practice of lesser painters. The architecture of a McFee canvas remains its dominant aspect, it gives his pictures their enduring charm.

But we have interrupted McFee's discussion of his creative procedure. "When I begin to paint," he tells us, "I place patches of color lightly touched-in on the important projections. Generally, these color tones are the half-tones just away from the highest light. These I use as tentative color 'anchors.' I then pro-

ceed quite rapidly to develop the color from dark to light throughout the canvas. I am not conscious of painting objects but kinds of color, and I am concerned with how the color develops. Objects take form almost of themselves and the aspect of the picture begins to emerge. I am always conscious of the necessity of preserving the picture plane. I do not desire to create the illusion of space but try rather to make the canvas tactile in every part—space to be realized as com-

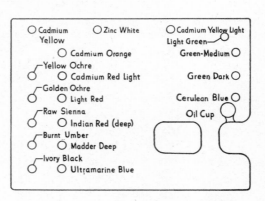

McFEE'S PALETTE

If you put the primary colors in a circle, you will have the spectrum or rainbow—from purple blue through the reds into the yellows and then the greens down to cerulean blue. McFee uses the earth colors and black to reinforce the true colors.

BLUE COMPOTE   OIL   24 x 30

STILL LIFE   OIL

pletely as the thing or object. Space becomes the thing; the thing the space."

The more we study McFee's canvases with this "space becomes the thing; the thing the space" idea in mind the more we sense how greatly the equal reality of the space that surrounds the objects and the objects themselves account for the great charm of the result. To let the eye roam over any one of his canvases searching out these space delights is to extract new values that enhance our pleasure in seeing.

McFee's technical approach is simple. He uses as little medium as necessary—a mixture of two-thirds turpentine and one-third oil; tries to keep the canvas wet as long as possible and paints thinly at first, applying heavier pigment as he proceeds.

He paints with "brights" bristle brushes, 3/4 inch, 5/8 inch and 3/8 inch—seldom anything larger. After the picture is "really going" he shifts to flat, short-haired camel's hair brushes, the same sizes as his bristle brushes. These, he declares, are a real pleasure to use —excellent for modeling.

During the early phases of his painting he gets more of the spirit, the "gesture" of the motif. Compare any two of the canvases reproduced to sense what he means by "gesture."

"Now I work more carefully," the painter notes, "to make my color sequences right and to shape the pieces. I want my picture to be full in color—rich and clear; and I desire to crowd into it all I sense of its inner meaning.

"From now on to the end, I work slowly, making little changes, painting pieces again and again. Sometimes a plan is successful from the beginning and then I may finish my picture in a week. At other times I can't make things fit, or perhaps the light has changed and I have endless difficulties. But I hold to my plan, and, with patience, work out the many changes necessary until at last it comes out."

Writing of McFee's work some time ago in *Magazine of Art,* Ernest Brace thus summed up his impressions:

"The way into a McFee picture is not an obvious, well-trodden path. To perceive fully its beauty and the loveliness of its contours one must forget the simple, bucolic pleasures of mere surface painting. His pictures are deep, often complex, and never quick, strong-arm impressions of an unexplored mood. Although beautiful in color and technically brilliant, there is always emphasis upon form. They have in them the carefully planned grace and the completed thought of a successful sonnet."

William Palmer

NOVEMBER SNOW 1950

William Palmer

explorer of the mystery and wonder of life

I KNOW how easy it is to be extravagant after such a stimulating two-day visit as I had with the Palmers at their home in Clinton, New York, but William Palmer is really an extraordinary person and I have no fear of having my enthusiasm criticized by the many readers who know the man as well as his work.

It is sometimes said that what an artist *is* doesn't matter, that he should be judged by his work alone. That is a narrow point of view. It overlooks the truism that the greatest art of all is the art of living. If more present-day artists were vital as persons and significant as citizens in their communities, there would be far less complaint of the public's apathy toward art and its lack of respect for artists.

William Palmer always has had an unusual attitude toward art as a profession. In his youth he never thought of himself as a second Rembrandt; he never expected to be much noticed in the world of art; he never dared hope to make a living by painting pictures. Even today, though rated among America's top painters, and probably selling as well as most, he prefers not to *depend* upon picture sales. He believes that good painting cannot be produced with one eye on the canvas and the other on the customer.

No, Palmer is not a rich man's son. He inherited no fortune. He didn't marry a wealthy woman, although Catherine Wechsler, who became his wife in 1939, brought a dowry of considerably more value to an artist than a safety deposit vault full of stocks and bonds. He has always had to work for a living. Mural decoration and teaching have largely provided him with security and complete freedom to paint what he likes and the way he likes.

So Palmer is not among those who are always grumbling about a society that withholds its patronage. "How many people in the entire country," he asks, "really care whether any of us paints a single picture?" And he adds, "What of it? The sheer satisfaction we get from painting ought to be compensation enough."

He has not been tempted to continue production of a kind of canvas that may have made a strike with critics and the public. His work is constantly undergoing change, keeping pace with a sensitive mind that is in perpetual ferment and that reacts wholeheartedly to every new environment in which life's vicissitudes place him.

Thus we see several phases, or periods in his work that coincide with his changes in residence—Iowa, Canada, the Southwest and now Oneida County, New York. It is not merely that his pictures of these regions mirror their divergent visual aspects: each seems to have opened a new door to perception, each appears to have radically reorientated his vision.

Like all painters—certainly those with academic training—Palmer's earliest work was much concerned with surface appearance. With the years, his preoccupation with intangibles has grown deeper. His latest canvases are in a definitely mystical vein. They strive to express things felt rather than seen and they rely more upon symbolism than upon natural effect.

This does not mean that Palmer is less influenced by nature; he is more than ever under her spell: his thinking and his painting are wholly inspired by nature. He lives in the Oriskany Valley of New York, where the

INDIAN SUMMER   1938   14 x 30

seasons are changeable and greatly varied. There are the dramatic contrasts of cold, stormy winters and hot summers. That part of the country is extremely interesting geologically and affords the artist great pleasure in exploration.

On his four rural acres there are old apple trees and gardens where Palmer grows vegetables, fruits and flowers and where, as he says, many of his picture ideas germinate and grow. In the winter, he nurses a great variety of potted plants that occupy windows and nooks in nearly every room in his rambling hundred-year old Victorian house.

Discussing his latest work he said, "My recent search, to a large extent, has been in the concentration of the minute. I have been looking into the crevices of things and from my exploration of the small have gained a truer sense of the large. It is mystery and wonder, the earth forces that underlie surface appearance, which stimulate me to creative work."

A canvas called *The Source* seems to symbolize Palmer's preoccupation with the beginnings and the heart of things. It depicts a tiny waterfall, a mere trickle splashing upon the rocks—the beginning of a mighty river that goes down to the sea. The whole picture is actuated by the idea, designed to express the painter's fascination with nature's agelong processes.

I cannot help being reminded by Palmer of Henry Thoreau and would not have been surprised to see the following quotation from *Walden* tacked on the studio wall: "Shall I not have intelligence with the earth? Am I not partly leaves and vegetable mould myself?"

At any rate, "intelligence with the earth" is a prerequisite with Palmer; it is what gives vitality and meaning to all that flows from his brush. It makes a deal of difference to him whether the bones of mother earth are barely covered by a thin skin of vegetation as in the hills of Oneida County or are buried under five feet of Iowa's fertile soil. The country that he paints must first be explored, lived in and pondered until its character and its moods are as familiar as those of an old friend. He has to discover the essence of a place before he can paint it.

Thus we are not surprised to learn that, when he went from Iowa to Canada in 1930, he continued while there to paint his native land—drought pictures of Iowa—rather than the less familiar terrain which he had before his eyes. As a matter of fact, he never paints directly from nature—he experiences it. The only graphic work done outdoors is largely confined to pencil or fountain-pen scribbles in little sketchbooks—"notes," he calls them. Most of these are wholly unintelligible to anyone else, though for him they are

NORTHERN TWILIGHT   1942   15 x 17

definite records of observations and impressions. Often, among them will be careful drawings of a plant, a tree or a rock formation.

Many of his pictures grow out of pleasure excursions with friends, picnicking in the woods, swimming at the beach, golfing or exploring the great variety of geological formations which give his country its character. That is another opportunity for experiencing nature. On his sallies into the countryside he jots down his notes of whatever the event offers—groups of figures at play or at rest, relationships of figures to the landscape; the latter particularly, since the relationship of man to nature is the motivation of most of his pictures. And in these his aim is to induce the observer to identify himself with the picture personages rather than to observe them objectively; a pleasant experience in any Palmer canvas in which the present anxieties of a troubled world do not intrude.

Many of those on-the-spot scribbles or notes later become motives for canvases. First, however, their possibilities are tested in drawings. These are more apt to be abstract constructions or basic designs for pictures, rather than anything approaching finished drawings. They collect by the dozen in his studio and eventually a few of them become subjects for paintings. When he does make a "finished" drawing he never

translates that subject into a painting because, as he says, "A drawing is a complete expression." For him, it has exhausted the subject's possibilities.

It will be noticed that the sun or the moon is present in many of Palmer's canvases, and that the sky usually plays a prominent part in his picture's design. This, naturally, refers to those subjects where the sky is a dominant element as it is at the seashore and on the western plains. The turbulent hills of his present locality now command his interest and crowd the sky. Their rhythms and their rounded forms fill his canvases with violent movement and strident pattern. These, however, do not divert him from such quiet and poetic essays as *Fertile Night,* a small moonlit picture in which two sleepy horses stand silent under an old apple tree. The foreground is dotted with white flowers and the tiny points of light made by fireflies which, according to theory, fertilize the blossoms by night.

Palmer's canvases, it will be noted, frequently are very small. The lovely *Northern Twilight,* for example, is but 15 x 17 inches. These should not be thought of as less serious essays than the larger pictures —they require just as much time for germination and production. He likes to vary both size and proportion in order to avoid any tendency to formularize his designs. But whatever the proportion of the picture it

93

SNOW RIDGE 1947 13 x 22

usually starts with a "core," a controlling detail in the exact center where the diagonals cross. This, he explains, is in no sense a center of interest, but it is an area of indispensable interest around which the rest of the picture develops. In his pictures he does not strive for a *center* of interest because he wants to lead the observer throughout the landscape to discover the many points of interest which he believes should enliven every part of the design.

It was while he was in Canada in 1930 that the painter discovered he was a "dry" worker, that the medium which dried at once and permitted immediate overpainting was best suited to his temperament. Thus he began his experiments with tempera, the medium he has continued to prefer. This he employs in underpainting all his canvases which finally are completed with oil glazes.

"Painting in tempera," Palmer insists, "is not a difficult procedure if one simplifies one's formulas as much as possible and does not consider it essential to have a special painting technique to be used for this method only. The special advantage of tempera is that it dries and sets rather quickly, allowing one to continue with the picture until it is completed. Simplicity is the keynote—simplicity in the grounds, in the colors, in the medium and in the painting procedure. It is wise to have a well-considered sketch before one begins the painting: egg emulsion tempera does not lend itself amiably to trial-and-error painting. The glazes dry in 24 to 36 hours, unless one desires a slower-drying medium.

"To those who first attempt to work in tempera, do not be afraid of the medium, paint freely and with spirit. Most people feel that painting in tempera is allied to a style of painting. This is not the case; tempera may be employed in any of the various schools of painting. It may be applied broadly or with small brush strokes, and impasto may be achieved if it is built-up carefully. Egg-oil emulsion tempera must not be confused with the pure egg tempera used by the Italian primitives which, because of the nature of that medium, calls for a smaller approach than oil emulsion, which is broad. The beauty of tempera is that it always remains permanent and is probably the only white which never changes over a period of years. A limited palette gives one greater freedom. Painting in tempera calls for a sensible choice of a few related colors. Beautiful results may be achived through the optical effects of one color underneath another.

"I have found, over a period of years, that the egg-oil emulsion tempera is the best and, with it, I recommend the use of titanium white which not only is very hard but also has great opacity. Zinc white is much too thin a white to be employed, since it is so transparent and weak in its covering properties. If one cannot get titanium dioxide white, then white lead powder (cremnitz white) can be used, but it is poisonous and must be handled with care. Egg emulsion tempera may be painted on an oil canvas which has been given a coat of varnish glaze. The tempera is painted into it while the varnish glaze is still tacky. If all of the materials and formulas are in order, egg emulsion dries and sets almost immediately.

"I have found it wise to make a preliminary painting on the ground, then to leave it for an indefinite length of time and, after it is entirely dry, to continue the overpainting. My first painting in tempera dries overnight in good weather; that is, if the ground is right. In damp weather the drying takes longer.

"Titian, who was a great craftsman, is said to have kept six or seven paintings around his studio in different stages of development, and to have worked on them daily over a period of time. This system gives you constant variety in your working problems since some paintings will be in a preliminary stage, some half-finished, and others in need of only a few tender touches to complete them.

"I always make my own sun-thickened oil. Pure cold-pressed linseed oil is placed in a vessel with a piece of glass over it and left in the sun over a period of days until it has the consistency of thin honey. Oil placed in the sun in this manner does not turn dark even though it may stand around the studio for some time. I also recommend that the artist make his own damar varnish in order to have it the consistency he prefers. Place the damar crystals in a cheesecloth bag and suspend over turpentine in a mason jar with the cover screwed on tight. Damar crystals dissolve in twenty-four hours, leaving the residue in the cheesecloth bag. I usually use two parts turpentine to one part damar crystals. This makes a heavy varnish that can be diluted with rectified turpentine as needed. Venice turpentine is used in a glaze to slow up its drying and give it a more slippery quality. (Rubens followed this procedure.) I never employ a dryer of any kind in any of my work.

"Masonite pressed board is an excellent base for the ground. I use the smooth side of the board and roughen it with sandpaper or a vegetable grater. This makes a better surface for the gesso ground than would the rough side which is so mechanical in its effect. Five-ply wood is also good for a gesso panel, but those larger than 20 x 24 inches should be cradled on the back to prevent warping.

"I recommend cologne glue for grounds, but rabbit-skin glue (in sheets) is also good. For gesso panels on wood, french gelatine (in sheets) can be used. Gesso is made of one cup of guilders' whiting to one cup of glue size. This is for absorbent grounds. The panel is given one coat of glue size and then the first coat of thin gesso is applied and rubbed in thoroughly with the palm of the hand, followed by several additional coats of gesso.

"For painting in egg emulsion, I prefer to use a half-chalk ground. This can be made by tacking linen on a stretcher frame, giving the linen one very thin coat of size, then taking one measure of whiting, one of zinc, and one of glue size mixed together, and adding to it, drop by drop, not more than two-thirds of a measure of boiled linseed oil (the less oil the better). This makes a good absorbent ground, which is what tempera requires. Grounds made in this manner should powder off lightly if sandpapered. If, instead, they are polished by sandpapering, then the ground is too brittle and will easily crack.

LICHEN ON THE ROCKS   1947   30 x 20

"My formula for egg emulsion is 2 parts egg, 1 part sun-thickened oil, 1 part damar varnish 2:1 (made of 2 parts turpentine to 1 part damar crystal), and water up to and not more than, 3 parts. I always make my egg emulsion with an egg beater. Beat the egg well, mix the oil and varnish together thoroughly and add to the egg mixture; beat well, then add the water drop by drop. This will make a complete emulsion that merely needs to be agitated in a flask before it is used each day. It keeps very well—my emulsions have lasted in my studio for over a year with no preservative added. Test the emulsion by dropping it in water. If it diffuses, it is successful; if it floats on top, it has not been emulsified with the water. Powdered white should be ground with this medium to tube consistency.

"It is always wise to begin the painting much higher in key than that of the final effect desired. The secret of success in painting is to have the light behind, working to the dark.

"Since I employ the method of underpainting, I cover my ground with a thin damar varnish (4 parts turpentine, 1 part damar crystals) mixed with the color I want to paint against. Against this, I paint freely with the white, building up a brilliant underpainting. I then mix color with damar varnish that has a small quantity of oil in it, and paint quickly on top of the underpainting. Many interesting effects can be achieved in this way. Either a similar or an opposite color may be used as a base for the next color. It is wise to put on this thin veil of color only once. Too many of them make the painting weak and do not provide a firm base for the surface painting in oil. I employ powdered color throughout my work. I grind it with linseed oil to the right consistency and then use a painting medium of 1 part damar varnish (2 parts turpentine, 1 part damar crystals) to 1 part turpentine and 1 part sun-thickened oil. I add no dryer to this, and use venice turpentine only when I feel the need of a slower-drying medium. This oil glaze dries rapidly and does not remain tacky. The first glaze over tempera—for that matter, the original glaze over the ground itself—gives the effect of pastel paper. It should never appear glassy or brittle; if it does, there is too much damar varnish in it.

"The simpler the glaze, the less mistakes one is likely to make. It is never wise to paint with egg emulsion into a glaze formula which has slow-drying elements in it. Egg emulsion sets quickly and produces an insoluble layer on top of any previous coat. The only way the paint underneath can dry is through the pores of the egg emulsion film; therefore, the painting must dry before one continues.

"If one wishes to use venice turpentine, add one-half teaspoon to three ounces of the glaze medium, cover the dry painting with this glaze, remove excess with a rag, and then paint directly into this with color ground in oil.

The following rules just about sum up my painting procedure:

1. Firm, absorbent ground, free from dust and dirt; either gesso panel or half-chalk ground.
2. Isolate ground from painting. Paint should lie on surface and not sink into the ground. Use 1 part damar to 4 parts turpentine. Grind your color in this. Spread on ground with rag. This should leave a surface that gives the effect of pastel paper.
3. Paint into this with egg tempera emulsion in either monochrome or polychrome. Keep the underpainting high in key. This preliminary painting sets and dries overnight. However, it is best to let it dry longer if possible.
4. For overpainting, use powdered color ground with linseed oil or sun-thickened oil. (The latter dries more rapidly.) Mix with glaze medium, which is 1 part damar 2:1, 1 part sun-thickened oil, and 1 part turpentine. Mix glazes with this medium and stain underpainting.
5. If painting is not successful, use tempera emulsion again or complete the picture with powdered color and oil medium. Add more oil for each successive layer of oil paint. However, the painting dries more slowly with each added layer. A good rule to remember is fat on lean, dark on light, thick on thin, opaque on transparent, warm on cool. Do not paint too many layers. It is always wise to add a small amount of white to underlying glazes and complete the picture in pure transparent glazes."

William Palmer received his art training at the Art Students League of New York under Kenneth Hayes Miller, Thomas Benton and Boardman Robinson. In 1927 he went abroad, studied at L'École des Beaux Arts, at Fontainebleau, and traveled in Holland where the landscapes he had known only through Rembrandt, Ruisdael and other painters of the Low Countries, reminded him of his native Iowa and gave him added incentive to paint its fields and plains upon his return.

From Nicholas Poussin, Palmer learned much about the relation of figures to landscape. Lorraine and Turner influenced him as did Rubens and Titian, the latter being a continuous source of inspiration.

The European journey did much to orient the young painter whose interests up to then had been with the picturesque. Thenceforth, his search has been for the universal rather than the incidental and the unusual.

When Palmer returned to New York in 1931, Alan Gruskin became interested in him and gave him his first one-man show at Midtown Galleries. He was soon engaged in painting murals under the P.W.A.P. Later he became supervisor of the Mural Project of the W. P. A. in New York City. His murals are to be found in Queen's General Hospital, Jamaica, New York, and in the Post Office Department Building in Washington, D. C., a commission won in 1936 in a national competition under the aegis of the Fine Arts Division of the Treasury Department.

Later, Palmer joined the teaching staff of the Art Students League and became director of the Mural Program of the Beaux Arts Institute of Design and secretary of the National Mural Painters Society.

In 1941 he was invited to go to Utica to become director of the School of Art of the Munson-Williams-Proctor Institution—a position he still holds—and to serve as Artist-in-Residence at Hamilton College.

For two years during World War II he was in the Armed Forces of the United States.

William Palmer has been accorded various awards, including a medal in the Paris Salon of 1937, a prize in 1946 from the National Academy of Design, a gold medal in the Audubon Artists Exhibition, 1948, and the Jack Kriendler Memorial Award at the Salmagundi Club in the same year. As a native son he was honored by having a collection of his work incorporated in the opening exhibition of the Des Moines Art Center.

Palmer's pictures are in many public and private collections such as the Whitney Museum, the White House in Washington, D. C., Metropolitan Museum of Art, Addison Gallery of American Art, Cranbrook Museum, American Academy of Arts and Letters, Encyclopaedia Britannica Collection and the Munson-Williams-Proctor Institute.

Hobson Pittman

In this picture the artist is guided by a previous pastel study as he paints on his canvas. This is habitual practice. Most of his themes are first expressed in either pastel or watercolor—sometimes in both—before he essays his final and most serious interpretation in oil. Note the draperies hanging in the trees, a device frequently employed as a background accessory.

Hobson Pittman uses a limited palette of great richness; warm grays, a wide range of clear blues, fresh greens, deep reds and occasional intense yellows and oranges.

Hobson Pittman

painter of romance and fantasy

SOME painters are born realists; others find maturity in the romantic realm of their imaginations, flavored occasionally, as in the art of Hobson Pittman, with strange nostalgic fantasy.

Warm glow of lighted interiors against cool moonlight seen through open doors and huge windows is Hobson Pittman's favorite color motif. Add a passion for things Victorian and for memories of a childhood lived in the post-Civil War environment of stern dignity and you have an almost complete catalogue of Pittman's creative sources. Such human interest as creeps incidentally into many of his canvases stems from the same source. The ghostlike women who inhabit his pictures are memories of frail spinsters who were the lavender-and-old-lace of horse-and-buggy days. Among these were *Miss Pat and Miss Eva Lion,* next door neighbors to the Pittmans, pictured in a large and exquisite canvas of that title. The only function of these apparitions would seem to be to enhance the quality of loneliness that is the atmosphere of Pittman's moody art; they play little or no part in the purely sensual qualities of his canvases. In his early pictures the rooms were invariably unoccupied—even by ghosts—and the artist became known as a "painter of the empty room." Some one added the significant phrase: "With the sense of presence withdrawn but briefly." The rocker on the porch, the divan facing the open doors, the cavernous beds—though empty—seemed indeed to convey the sense of human proximity.

Seldom has a painter reflected the influences of his youth so faithfully. Hobson Pittman was born on a farm in Tarboro, North Carolina, in 1900, where he lived until he was ten years of age. The family then moved to the village into a large, rambling, three-story Victorian house with high ceilings and very tall windows, the latter opening onto a porch which surrounded all four sides. Relatives, whom he visited for several years, lived in similar houses of the period, furnished with handsome and—to the future painter— "strange" pieces of Victorian furniture.

Pittman became thoroughly imbued with the spirit of these surroundings, and even their details were indelibly photographed upon his impressionable brain. The theme of the double doors opening out onto a porch flooded with moonlight has been repeated, with variations, in many canvases. *Southern Mansion,* a canvas painted prior to *Miss Pat and Miss Eva Lion,* has the identical setting, a wavy-backed divan occupying the same position in the room as the piano.

Bedrooms have had a special appeal. "I remember," says Pittman, "how the beds in these North Carolina homes were pulled out in the middle of the rooms on hot summer nights. This was the customary thing to do. I recall with what fascination, at an early age, I watched my sisters and my aunts strolling around the bedrooms in their long, white nightgowns." In his canvas, *Four a.m.,* Pittman has painted the lamp still burning after the occupant of the room has gone to bed. This, he says, was his sister Lena's custom. The light gave her a sense of security even though doors and windows were wide open.

In *The Invalid,* Pittman employs every artifice at his command to create a mood of loneliness and pathos. There is the vast, threatening expanse of sea, and the unfriendly sky into which death stares from the invalid's chair. It is a picture that in contemplation awakens the primitive emotions of apprehension and the sense of man's insignificance before nature's threatening forces. Says the artist: "The memory of the long, endless sweep of the boardwalk has haunted me since, long ago, I first saw it at the seashore. I've made many, many sketches of this theme, first in pencil, then in pastel. The wheel chair that had haunted my memory since childhood days, when I often stood and stared at it in awe, seemed to introduce itself into the theme."

Pictures that are born of such broodings are of long gestation. Years often elapse between conception and final realization. *Summer Pleasures,* completed in 1945, was started in 1937. The picture passed through various experimental stages. At first the figure in the rocking chair was seen dimly behind a transparent screen. When the screen was removed, the drapery in the trees was added.

It will be seen that in these canvases the artist is indifferent to scale, proportion and perspective as commonly conceived. In *Summer Pleasures,* for example, the relation of the hammock and the rocking chair violates physical possibility. Although the hammock hangs from a tree behind the chair, it is nearer the spectator. The flouting of scale is dramatically illustrated in *Miss Pat and Miss Eva Lion,* the open door being large enough to admit a locomotive. The device of this ex-

MISS PAT AND MISS EVA LION   OIL

A large canvas, contrasting the warm interior (intensely red rug) with the blue night sky. The piano is bright red. The chairs are blue, bringing the cool hues of the sky into the lighted room. The ghostlike figures, Miss Pat and Miss Eva Lion, are romantically remembered spinster neighbors.

SUMMER PLEASURES OIL

Begun in 1937, this picture was on Pittman's easel, off and on, for seven years.

THE INVALID

OIL

A small canvas in cool and low-toned colors.

aggeration serves Pittman's purpose well. It has the same effect of subordinating mere human beings to awesome nature as the dwarfing of the figures in his canvas, *The Invalid.*

When Pittman left the South to establish himself in Pennsylvania he brought his memories with him. At first they were less insistent, and while he has never fallen under the influence of any other painter to the extent of imitation, his early one-man exhibitions in Philadelphia revealed a distinct kinship with the art thought of Charles Burchfield. The urge was not inconsistent, since Burchfield, like Pittman, has been haunted by Victorian relics. They were then, however, even in Pittman's work, hard relics with none of the soft, romantic pigments and blendings characteristic of the later work.

Unlike painters who know exactly what they want and where they are going before they touch brush to canvas, Pittman allows himself to live within his dream and to develop a painting as that dream may dictate in process of working.

"I have a veritable fountain of ideas in my mind all at the same time," says this painter of subtle fantasies, "many more than I can put on canvas, but once an idea becomes dominant I have to paint it.

"When I stop painting on a picture I don't exhibit it for at least a year, but keep it in my studio. After I have put it away for a while I look at it again and almost always take something out or put something in.

"Most people," he claims, "would think I was crazy to have so large a palette. It is thirty years old, too. I like it for its fine patina. Right now I am trying to break in a new palette, but I just can't make myself use it because it lacks what the old one has.

"I pay more attention to earth colors than to any others, since they neutralize color and, in consequence, a painting becomes more luminous. I keep my palette clean," says the painter whose studio, in contradiction, is cluttered with all sorts of objects and sketches, "I don't like a surface all piled up with gooey pigment."

He uses many flat bristle brushes, never round ones, and few small ones. Before he starts a picture he makes innumerable sketches. These he lays out on the floor and pins to the wall in front of him so that he can start "building them into a painting."

Like a stage manager he has props which he terms his "library of ideas." In this library are hundreds, if not thousands, of careful drawings made over the years as he sees something that arrests his attention. On trips back to North Carolina, for instance, he has made any number of careful sketches showing pieces of Victorian furniture, expressive groupings of furniture, and the layout of interiors. Later he uses these as sets to be peopled by his strange, lonely figures—the invalid on the boardwalk wistfully gazing toward the horizon, or thin black-clad women in a stark stair-walls-and-doors hallway that might well be the epitome of all old ladies' homes.

When a picture begins to jell in his mind, Pittman first draws it in with charcoal or perhaps with pastel to get the color. To such an extent does the idea possess him that he gets up in the middle of the night to put down on his canvas the thoughts that have kept him awake. But in spite of his innumerable preliminary sketches he never finishes a canvas as he visualized it at the start.

"If I like a subject," he says, "I don't care what anyone else may say about it." Changes thus come from within, not from without.

Pittman stretches and sizes his canvas himself; using, of course, the very best canvas. "After sizing the canvas," he explains, "it is allowed to dry for six or eight weeks. Then a tone of pale yellow-gray earth color takes the white glare away. I never work directly on white canvas. Finally, I varnish the surface with retouching varnish that helps to hold the drawing in

place when I begin to paint. I do not trace a cartoon on a canvas because I keep making changes as I go along. The idea is premeditated, but organization is tentative and develops as I work on the canvas."

Pittman relies on his many sketches of objects for foreground realism and uses landscape largely as binder for atmospheric suggestion and support.

"I feel deeply every stroke I put on canvas," he declares. "I first started to paint when I was eleven, and came North when I was seventeen. In my twenties I did a whole series of abstract oils and gouaches. Deep down in my heart I am still absorbed with abstract and non-objective painting," he continued, nodding toward the color reproductions of work by Braque and Picasso hanging on his walls.

"My own things are really seen and built up abstractly. I do feel beyond what the eye sees, and, from my own experience, believe that if I *feel* rhythm, balance and space, they'll come. Otherwise, they won't."

Pittman keeps two or three canvases going simultaneously to allow the surfaces to dry thoroughly before he begins to repaint. "In the morning," he says, "I may like a picture, but at noon I'll think it's horrible!"

As a painter, Pittman likes to retire within himself. Years ago, the "folksiness" of other artists so disturbed him that now he keeps his studio door closed against intrusion and never allows anyone to see a picture while he is in the process of painting it.

"Every year," he insists, "I feel more and more like a student, but I don't believe, as some do, that you must always be changing your style or your technique— switch, for instance, from one medium to another. It has taken me all these years to learn the little I know now, and the business of starting all over would seem too much of a mountain for me."

Pittman received his training at Rouse Art School in North Carolina, Pennsylvania State College, Carnegie Institute of Technology, Columbia University, and through travel abroad where he studied in important museums and galleries during 1928, 1930, 1935 and 1948. His honors include honorable mention at the San Francisco World's Fair, 1939, and at the Butler Art Institute, 1943; a Purchase Prize from the Virginia Museum of Fine Arts, 1940; the Scheidt Memorial Prize at the Pennsylvania Academy of the Fine Arts the same year, the Dawson Memorial Medal from that institution, 1944; second prize in the San Francisco American Exhibition, 1947; Clark Prize at the Corcoran Gallery of Art, 1948; and third prize at the Carnegie Institute's "Painting in the United States, 1949" exhibition.

His work is owned by most of the country's major museums, and appears in such other collections as those of Pennsylvania State College, International Business Machines, Encyclopaedia Britannica Collection and Pepsi-Cola. Pittman is head of the Art Department at Friends Central County and Day School in Pennsylvania and he teaches at the summer sessions of Pennsylvania State College.

OPPOSITE: *Pencil studies for "Warm Evening" (see color plate) and "The Invalid."*

Iver Rose

"HI YA, FOLKS"   OIL

Iver Rose

painter with a radiant brush

IVER ROSE builds up his pictures so expertly in color and texture that every square inch abounds in sensuous delight. It is evident that, like Chardin, he handles paint as though he loves it for its own sake. As one critic wrote, "Rose's unique worth lies in the magic he achieves with the painted surface." "Glamorous" color, "lush" color, "electric" color, "luminous flashes," "textures that remind us of fine and intricate embroideries" are among the expressions often used to define the qualities that characterize his canvases.

This surface radiance is, indeed, what first impresses us in all of his work, but the quality of Rose's canvases is more than skin deep. Although in most of them form seems considerably camouflaged by overlapping color planes and lost contours, they are thoughtfully and solidly constructed. His modeling is, of course, suggestive of Cézanne whom he acknowledges as his most revered master. Cézanne's dictum "Where there is fullness of color there should be fullness of form" comes to mind as we note Rose's substitution of bright color for conventional shadow treatment.

As to all-over picture structure, Rose lays out his designs with the percipience of a first-rate lyric abstractionist. His pictures all start with line scribbles which seek the most expressive line and space analysis for the particular subject. Says Rose, referring to his first adventures in painting, back in the early thirties, "The abstract quality of Cézanne's work entirely engrossed me and I studied his paintings assiduously. At the same time I was dissecting the works of the old masters, bringing them down to their abstract elements. It was through these experiments that I discovered that the same geometric structure is to be found in both the old and the new masters. The great contribution which moderns have made to art, in my opinion, is the rediscovery of the geometric structure and abstract elements to be found in all great works produced through the ages."

A characteristic of Rose's canvases which cannot be demonstrated in black-and-white reproductions is the dramatic emphasis in abstract backgrounds of the subject's action and mood. Emily Genauer expressed this very well in her comment upon *Sharp Drummer* "in which the ecstatic figure and his vibrating traps—the cymbals are an explosion of brassy-yellow pigment—are a perfect synthesis of jazz music." It will be seen—even in our halftone—how the background of *Balancing Act* is designed to express the balancing action of the performer, and the feeling of vertigo induced by his act.

Preoccupied, as we are apt to be, with the technical brilliance of Rose's work, we might easily slight its human aspect. Although the man does indeed love paint for its own sake, he has a humanity-loving consciousness and his incentives spring from his interests in people, all kinds of people, but principally the little people who toil at common tasks. The fisher-folk of Rockport have inspired many of his canvases. Rose has summered in this little fishing port on the Massachusetts coast since 1930 and he is thoroughly conversant with its picturesque scenes and its human drama.

Hauling in Nets, Docking, Waiting (fishermen's wives awaiting the arrival of the fleet), *Fishermen's Casualty,* and *Gloucester Gossips* are some of the paintings that have their source in this colorful harbor village. Quarry men and miners have been dramatically portrayed by Rose's brush, as have the pretzel woman, hokey-pokey man, flower vendor, and hurdy-gurdy player. His treatment of these subjects is tragic or whimsical according to their nature. In all, his role is that of the kindly philosopher who smiles—but with sympathy—at the amusing things people do and are. He is in no sense a propagandist, nor a satirist; there is no acid in his commentaries

Although not a musician himself, Rose is a lover of music and he is fascinated by musicians, especially by amateurs whose enthusiasm in their efforts is so naïve and obvious—a thumping, banging boogie-woogie player crouching over the keyboard, a tousle-headed youngster *blowing it out* of a saxophone, a bus driver sawing away at a bull fiddle against a background of orange-red rhythms. One canvas depicts a triangle player, his rod held to his lips as he follows the illuminated score on his music-stand, waiting throughout an entire symphony for the right instant when a single "ping" on his steel will begin and end his performance.

I find a key to the character of Iver Rose in his experience back in 1929-30 during his transition from one way of life to another. It is difficult to imagine the Iver Rose of today as a top-flight commercial artist, making newspaper drawings for New York's big department stores—but that was his life for fifteen years, in what might be called his first incarnation. It was not the kind of life he would have chosen had he been free to choose, and throughout those years he dreamed of that "some day" when, with accumulated savings, he could retire and take up his brushes. It was the ill wind of 1929's economic crash that practically blew him into his career as a painter. His savings wiped out, he decided it was

BOBBY SOCKS   OIL

This jolly picture of high school girls in their babushkas is cast in a high key, with yellows and oranges predominating.

Black-and-white reproductions of Iver Rose's pictures are particularly inadequate because his shadows are usually painted in fairly bright color rather than the conventional value treatment.

BLOWING IT OUT   OIL

CLOWN'S HEAD   OIL

WAITING OIL 22 x 30

The monumental construction of this picture is expressive of its theme—fishermen's wives stoically watching the horizon for the return of the fleet.

now or never. He "chucked all commercial work overboard" and went back to Chicago, the place of his birth. He rented a studio and "furnished it with a couch, an easy chair and a box of cigars." Says Rose, "For a full year I smoked cigars and read books, mostly standard works of literature from which I learned more about art than from any art books I have studied. During an entire year I didn't touch a brush. I just wanted to have time to think, to get all those years of commercialism out of my system and soak up all I could of the meaning of art in its relation to life."

Profitable to the inner man as was this transition period, its memory is a recitation of hardships that must have been trying to one accustomed to good living. "My little savings," he recalls, "were in constant flight and quickly gone. I found myself living in lofts, shacks, and garrets. I became intimately familiar with eviction laws, the cheapest grease joints and marketplaces. But I was sustained by my love of art, my unquenchable desire to paint, and by a mirth that was as great as my girth (I tipped the scales at 300, more or less, and it wasn't all muscle). The girth proved to be something of a blessing; it enabled me to survive long, forced dieting without physical harm."

BALANCING ACT OIL 32 x 20

This canvas is designed to express the balancing action of the performer and the feeling of vertigo induced by his act.

109

Rose began to paint in 1930. He also took up lithography for which he first became known in the art world. But after a few years he gave up black and white entirely, because he felt it was having a deleterious effect upon his color. His painting quickly won recognition. Exhibition followed exhibition and in a few years he was counted among America's "best knowns." His pictures found their way into the museums and private collections.

To return to "paint quality" and technical procedures, it should be noted that Rose achieves his vibrant coloration by means of repeated overpaintings. Examining his canvases closely we can see how he has glazed a rich orange with a brilliant blue passage, a green with a purple. His glazes are opaque. The pigment, with little or no medium—a petroleum retouch varnish —is dragged on in broken tones which permit the undercolor to shine through, a method at variance with the usual glazing practice of flowing on transparent color that practically covers the undercoat.

This painting procedure implies a very slow maturing of the canvas. Each application of color requires a long time for thorough drying before it is ready to receive more paint. It is not surprising, therefore, to learn that most of Rose's pictures are about two years in the making and that many canvases are being carried on simultaneously. Rose believes that this gradual development of his pictures is creatively wholesome, because each picture has the advantage of a "fresh eye" every time it comes up for additional painting.

There is great variety in Rose's color schemes which are "cast," as he puts it, to characterize the particular subject. *Bobby Socks,* for example, is cast in a high key in which yellows and oranges predominate; *Waiting,* a sombre subject, has a dominance of dark blues, browns and oranges—all colors muted.

Rose's palette is a sheet of milk glass, thirty inches square, on his painting stand. His colors around three sides are, in the following order: white, cadmium yellow, cadmium orange, cadmium red, yellow ochre, burnt umber, venetian red, ultramarine blue, light green, veridian, monastral green, burnt sienna, black, alizarin crimson (the last named, used sparingly as a glaze, or alone).

Rose does much of his painting with a palette knife. A collection of much-worn brushes, that would be the despair of a Taubes or a Speicher, serve for the rest.

Most of the pictures are small. They range from 8 x 10 to 22 x 36. It is his quite common practice to paint small studies preparatory to developing the large canvases.

Iver Rose, at 50, is in the prime of his career. He is making an important contribution to the tradition of fine painting. He is represented in the collections of the Addison Gallery of American Art, Cranbrook Museum, Witte Memorial Museum, Museum of the New Britain Institute, University of Georgia, Walker Art Center, the Encyclopaedia Britannica Collection, Fine Arts Gallery of San Diego, the American Academy of Arts and Letters, and in the private collections of Paul Gardner, Mrs. Otto Spaeth, Mrs. Herman Shulman and Mr. and Mrs. M. Neumann.

Charcoal study (6 x 8) for "In the Gallery" (see color plate).

Andrée Ruellan

NOMADS OIL 38 x 30

Andrée Ruellan
painter of the color and pageantry of life

I FIRST MET Andrée Ruellan on a July morning when, stepping from a bus that had brought me to Woodstock, I saw her, petite, brunette and altogether charming, standing beside John W. Taylor, her tall painter husband. They had driven into town to meet me for a visit long planned and now at last materialized.

Woodstock, New York, is the home of many famous painters. The town lies in a beautiful valley of Ulster County. It is dominated by Overlook Mountain which often hides its head in the clouds for days on end. Roads leaving the town center lead to homes and studios hidden in the enfolding hills. In the village itself many ancient houses have sprouted telltale skylights. The Ruellan-Taylors live beyond Shady, a hamlet on the edge of Woodstock. A drive of a few miles up the Sawkill Valley brings one to their rural home, a tiny old house built into the side of a hill, just below Cooper Lake.

A little distance from their home the Taylors have built their studios. At first a single studio served both artists. Later enlargement provided each with separate quarters.

A first glance around Andrée's studio shows her to be an extremely well-organized craftsman. Although bulging with canvases, easels, portfolios and the usual studio clutter, all is orderly and shipshape.

On her easel that July day was a large canvas of a Savannah street scene, and on a wall were tacked numerous sketches and studies for the picture, in Wolff pencil and gouache.

Her palette, a 20 x 25 sheet of milk glass on a painting stand beside her easel, was set with nineteen colors. A handful of brushes lay on the table. In cabinets and on shelves against a wall her stock of equipment was neatly stored.

Andrée Ruellan is an objective painter. She is interested in the color and pageantry of life around her, wherever she may be. Yet, as she says: "People are never just spots of color. What moves me most is that in spite of poverty and the constant struggle for existence, so much kindness and sturdy courage remain. Naturally I want to paint well-designed pictures—but I also wish to convey these warmer human emotions. No ivory tower—I feel strongly that the artist is an important member of society, and he should do his part to build a world where war and poverty, as well as racial discrimination, are impossible. I want as good a technique as possible, but only for the purpose of expressing clearly, yet with subtlety, what I feel about life. My work can be no better than I am myself as a person, and no deeper than my understanding of life as a whole. It is true that I paint some landscapes and still lifes, but from the earliest drawings my deepest interest has been and is for people, at work or at play. It seems to me that it is in the most normal surrounding—a subway entrance, a marketplace or on the street—that one finds the unexpected in situation and aspect."

New York street scenes have been the subjects of some of Miss Ruellan's best canvases. She was born and lived for many years in the immediate vicinity of Washington Square, prior to going abroad. And it is there that she has returned every winter with one or two exceptions. Her canvas *Spring in Bleecker Street* was painted in her studio on the south side of the Square during the winter of 1938.

A considerable part of Miss Ruellan's work has its origin in the South, where the Taylors have gone repeatedly to visit relatives and to make intimate studies which have become the motive of so many of Miss Ruellan's most noteworthy pictures.

Then there is the circus, of which Miss Ruellan has done numerous canvases and drawings. When in Paris she went often to the Cirque d'Hive, and on her studio wall is pinned a press pass that attests the hours she has spent at Madison Square Garden in New York.

Wherever Miss Ruellan goes she carries her little black sketchbooks (about 5 x 7); in these she jots down impressions, details of things she may want to put in pictures, composition ideas for canvases, penciled color notations. It is interesting to thumb through these sketchbooks and discover direct-from-life sources of her well-known paintings.

Her pictures always begin with much preliminary study in lead pencil. Wolff pencil studies on large sheets follow, some details, other compositional experiments.

It is the artist's practice to develop her subjects in gouache before beginning work in oil. These are done on paper about 16 x 20 inches. While these color studies usually give a reasonably accurate forecast of the final rendering in oil, Miss Ruellan avoids carrying them so far as to exhaust or too greatly dilute her fresh incentive for the painting that is to follow. She often does more work on these gouaches after completing her painting on canvas, and they become finished pictures that are sometimes seen in exhibitions. But let us ask Miss Ruellan to tell in her own words something about her working methods:

"Usually I find it best to work on a number of canvases at the same time, setting aside a painting when the interest lags and the vision is not clear. I paint every day about six hours, with periods of outdoor sketching or a week or so of drawing in the studio.

"The best drawings seem to come after a few days of concentration in the medium, whether pure line in lead pencil or brush and chinese ink (ground from the stick and black stone). The later tonal drawings in Wolff pencil are generally studies for paintings, to complement the color sketch in gouache or oil.

"As for the paintings, I draw-in the composition lightly with charcoal and begin with very thin washes, using as medium about 10 parts double-rectified turpentine to 1 part sun-thickened linseed oil. With these light washes I try to approximate the final color scheme without extreme lights or darks. In this stage and when starting body color I sometimes use 1 part cremnitz tempera white (egg-oil-damar emulsion) to 3 parts cremnitz oil white to accelerate drying and to keep the paint 'lean.' The general color scheme established, blocking-in of the larger forms begins with body paint and increasing the oil content of the medium to 2 or 3 parts turpentine to 1 part linseed oil. The procedure in this middle stage varies according to size of picture and the individual forms—a large, simple sky is painted quite differently from one that is broken in forms and color. Also I try to keep in mind the final color effect, certain cool colors needing warm undertones. Some passages to be semi-transparent, others opaque. Above all, to preserve the unity and freshness of the original conception. As the painting nears completion, I use a damar medium (sun-thickened linseed oil-turps-damar-1-1-1) making the more subtle adjustments through little glazes, refinement of edges, etc.

"As already mentioned, I wish to keep my painting method as flexible as possible, varying it according to the needs of the partciular picture. After trying numerous methods this seems the best for my purpose. No doubt it will be modified in the future as vision demands. A good technique is one used for those ends."

Andrée Ruellan was born April 6, 1905, in New York, of French parents. Her art study began in Leo Lentelli's sculpture and Maurice Sterne's drawing classes at the Art Students League. In 1922 she went abroad on a scholarship to continue her study with Maurice Sterne in Rome. From 1923 to 1929 she lived and studied in Paris, except for one winter (1927-28) spent in New York. In 1929 she married John W. Taylor and returned with him to the United States. The Ruellan-Taylors then went to Woodstock where they established their permanent home.

"In my formative years," says Miss Ruellan, "it was

The frame on the easel was made by the Ruellan-Taylors. They make all their own frames.

RANDY, JULIE
AND JOHN
OIL   27 x 38

Courtesy Art Institute, Zanesville, Ohio

The subject of "Randy, Julie and John" was first developed as a 10 x 14 gouache color study (above right). This was followed by several composition studies in black and white. The drawing at the right, 19 x 25, done in carbon pencil rubbed with a stump, was one of these. The head reproduced above is an exact-size detail from the drawing.

115

SPRING IN BLEECKER STREET   OIL

my good fortune to meet three fine people. The first was Robert Henri, who made a lasting impression in spite of my very young age. The second was Maurice Sterne, a most stimulating teacher. And in 1927 when I met Carl Zigrosser in Paris, and he asked me to have an exhibition at the Weyhe Galleries in New York, a fine friendship began."

Andrée Ruellan's drawings and prints are almost as well-known as her paintings. Her lithographs have been prominent in the print market for some years. In these her subtle sense of humor often finds expression.

Although Andrée says, "I am still young enough to feel that most of my achievement lies ahead," her achievement to date has been impressive. She is represented in the permanent collections of the Metropolitan Musum of Art, Fogg Museum, Phillips Memorial Gallery, William Rockhill Nelson Gallery, Zanesville Ohio Art Institute, Whitney Museum, the Philadelphia Museum, Library of Congress, Newark Public Library, the University of Nebraska and the University of Georgia, Springfield (Massachusetts) Museum, Museum of the New Britain Institute, Norton Gallery of Art, Encyclopaedia Britannica Collection, and International Business Machines.

Among her honors are a $1000-Grant in Arts from the American Academy of Arts and Letters and National Institute of Arts and Letters (1945), and the Pennell Memorial Medal from the Pennsylvania Academy of the Fine Arts (1948), as well as a Medal of Honor and Purchase in Pepsi-Cola's "Paintings of the Year" exhibition. She has also executed two mural commissions under the U. S. Treasury's Section of Fine Arts.

Helen Sawyer

ARRANGEMENT WITH MOON   OIL

Helen Sawyer
a virile painter of life and nature

SLIGHT, dark-haired and endowed with a warm, out-giving personality, Helen Sawyer unquestionably is one of America's most gifted painters.

She is the wife of Jerry Farnsworth, whom she met on Cape Cod (Massachusetts) where both were students in one of Charles W. Hawthorne's painting classes. Now they have a charming house in North Truro on the Cape and another in Sarasota, Florida, where they spend the winter months. Together, in both places, they conduct painting classes during such time as can be spared from their own creative work which, of course, is most important to them. When I visited them in Sarasota, their new school studio, roomy and modern in design, had just been completed. Their own work is done in the second floor studio of their comfortable home which was designed and built largely by Jerry himself. It is situated on the bank of one of the many Florida bayous that reach inland from the sea and afford opportunity for sailing, fishing and swimming; activities the Farnsworths enjoy in leisure hours.

To be the guest of the Farnsworths for a day is to discover the key to the particular qualities that give their work distinction. One is impressed at once by Helen's buoyancy, her *joie de vivre*, her fascination with the varied manifestations of life and nature. And one is especially sensitive to the success that both husband and wife have made of the art of living. The demands which Helen's career put upon her time and energy have in nowise lessened her love of home and homemaking.

Helen, a descendant of New England seafaring families, was born in Washington, D.C. Her talent was obvious during her early childhood and it was enthusiastically fostered by her painter father, Wells M. Sawyer. Some of her childhood was spent in Scarboro-on-the-Hudson and later in travel abroad with her parents who lived for many years in Spain, where Helen acquired her predilection for Spanish dishes. In addition to being a student at the Hawthorne School, Helen studied at the Art Students League and the old Academy School in New York.

Helen's interest in subject matter encompasses landscape, marines, still life, flowers and circus folk. Since Sarasota is the winter quarters of the Ringling Brothers circus, their acrobats and clowns are frequently found posing in her studio, and Helen often is to be seen wandering among the tents and wagons of the "Big Show." Her circus pictures are among her best.

Up north on the Cape she naturally finds incentive in its rugged landscape and its windy shores and sea. She knows the Cape in all its varied moods because she has lived there through every season of the year. She has painted those sparkling days when the dry Easterly gives a pure, undiluted quality to the light; she has no less eagerly captured the effect of gray, stormy landscapes when a tempest is brewing and storm clouds scud across the sky. Always she paints to express a mood rather than to record a specific scene—spring rather than an orchard, the threat and fury of sea and sky rather than a particular place in time of storm. She is one of very few contemporaries who really paint the sky convincingly and with appreciation of its contribution to the mood of the subject. In many of her canvases, sky and land seem woven together in a unified and colored fabric. She sometimes uses a station wagon as an outdoor studio, as she did in painting *Sailors Take Warning*, during a three-day Northeaster in January. She parked the car on the cliff a hundred feet

FISHING BEFORE THE STORM   OIL   18 x 30

above the Atlantic where the gale tossed the old car about like a small boat at sea. Asked to describe her experiences in painting this canvas, Miss Sawyer said:

"I made first a small oil, then organized a larger painting which I started outdoors. To help with some of the structural detail of the tower, beacon and other elements, I made a few detail drawings as I went along, and also made sketches of earth contours, masses and renderings of weeds and grasses, with color notes in writing. These written notes on color crystallize the first impression more fully.

"The landscape as finally worked out became more strongly stated and dramatic than the sketch had been. I could have worked out the picture entirely in the studio but I preferred to keep it outdoors in its elements of cold and salt wind.

"Drawing the detailed red-and-white trusses of the radio beacon and construction of the tower was difficult with my large canvas billowing like a square sail. At this point I made more drawings and decided to finish the canvas in the old station wagon, though there I had to work on my knees.

"In this lighthouse painting I tried to suggest the presence of the unseen ocean beyond the drop of the lighthouse buildings."

(Cape Cod Light, the subject of this canvas, is the oldest of Cape lights and one of the great beacons of the Atlantic Coast. The light is officially recorded as visible twenty miles at sea. It has been reported as seen forty-five miles at sea. Although Cape Cod Light is its official name, Cape Codders call it High-Land Light with emphasis on both syllables.)

From Cape Cod to Sarasota one encounters a dramatic change of scene, but Helen Sawyer paints Florida somewhat in the same mood as she does Cape Cod, seeking out the unspoiled elemental phases, the ever-changing skies and sea. You will find no tourists or waving palms on sandy beaches, but rather the back country of primitive forests with Negroes fishing on the edge of the shore and swamp, a blue-green lagoon known only to fishermen and sea birds. These are her subjects. She paints the Florida that is seldom seen or noticed by the average visitor. She has discovered that much of it is a primitive Eden still.

"Most of my landscapes," Helen says, "are only started after I have looked at the subject matter or pieces of it for days, weeks and sometimes years. By the time I paint the thing itself, its significance, its salient color relationships, and its mood are so much a part of me that I can think of the painting as a manifestation of life and the natural world, and the subject as notes and indexes to procedure. This is a curious psychological reversal which identifies the artist closely with his work and, strangely enough, allows great freedom of expression."

Miss Sawyer has no stereotyped way of planning a picture. Once launched, she works in the same manner on a landscape, still life, figure or a purely imaginative subject. Sometimes she makes pencil sketches of projected works, sometimes she begins by doing a small canvas of the idea. She likes to paint in oil on paper for such preparatory studies, a technique that she finds very sympathetic at the beginning. She explains, "These paintings are more than shorthand. To be valu-

SAILORS TAKE WARNING   OIL   36 x 42

THE CLOWN   OIL   30 x 25

"The wonderful clown, Buzzie Potts, was only able to pose for a little over half a day. This picture thus far remains a large sketch which has the tragic bright color and childlike good humor of the clown."

BAREBACK RIDER   OIL   30 x 25

able they have to convey the essence of all the structure needed in the picture—what is growing in this and that patch; why the sand looks darker here or there, or wetter; if deer moss or dried fern gives a certain hollow its peculiar color and texture; how the wind is blowing and if it smells of sand or bay or a distant fox.

"Sometimes a fleeting effect in nature that is passing quickly, overwhelmingly appeals to a knowledge and an impulse already formed; then the moment must be seized. In *Fishing Before the Storm* (a Florida subject) I saw the wonderful darkling light on the water almost at the end of day. The relationship between the pale shingle, pink and gray sky and the sea was so fine that I immediately made a small oil sketch, working as quickly as possible to recapture the real mood and color relationships. Months later, while in the prairie state of Illinois, I made the larger painting, using this sketch as a key."

In painting still life, a set-up is made after trying various arrangements of objects and background angles. Helen prefers a side light so that there are strong contrasts of light and dark. Usually the still life is organized around one relationship of two pieces of form and color coming together which has that abstract significance (or fascination) which gives the key to the whole and determines what and where the rest of the arrangement is finally composed.

She says that this early vision of key and mood of a particular canvas must be sustained through the various stages or else it becomes a perfunctory piece of craftsmanship and should be destroyed.

ANTHONY DRAWING 15 x 11

The artist draws directly on the canvas with lines of thinned paint, using ultramarine warmed with umber or other earth color and keeping the whole mobile as she works from one balancing part to another, thus becoming so familiar with the various parts and mood of the whole that it becomes like a world in itself which the painter inhabits.

Next she paints in solid color the richest darks, and next a passage here and there of light and color in small areas, weaving back and forth in working so that the canvas would look unintelligible to anyone but a painter while it is being developed.

"In doing *Mardi Gras*," says Miss Sawyer (see color plate), "I carried around in my head the scheme with rich blacks and the mood of the lady, then made a 14 x 16 oil on canvas in my Massachusetts studio. It was in Florida that I elaborated the conception of her and painted the larger one in a mood of dreaming up something delicious in color, iridescent and piquant."

Helen Sawyer has not confined her expression to one medium. She employs oil, watercolor and casein to suit the special purpose each medium will best serve. But it is in her oils that she excels. She has done some notable lithographs, too, and she has exhibited drawings that demonstrate both her power and her imagination.

Helen Sawyer is represented in many museum collections including the Whitney Museum of American Art, the Pennsylvania Academy of the Fine Arts, Toledo Museum, Indianapolis Museum and the Library of Congress.

The Farnsworth winter home is on a bayou near Sarasota, Florida. Winter quarters of the Ringling Circus are nearby and clowns, acrobats and other performers can often be found posing in Helen's studio.

Frederic Taubes

FIGURE LEANING   OIL   30 x 25

Frederic Taubes
a painter noted for creative power and craftsmanship

Taubes prepares just about all the materials that are used in the craft of painting. Here he mixes ingredients for a special kind of varnish.

FREDERIC TAUBES, an American of foreign birth, is making a considerable contribution to the development of contemporary painting in this country. His influence has two sources: the esthetic content of his art and his authority as a craftsman.

There is not much that could be said here on the spiritual aspect of his work which would add one whit to the reader's enjoyment of his pictures. When it comes to craftsmanship a lot can be said, and should be said because through want of sound craftsmanship much good painting of the past has perished with its creators, and many worthy canvases produced today are doomed to an early demise. This is not surprising because, as Taubes says in his, *You Don't Know What You Like:* "The education [today] of a painter-to-be is, as a rule, sketchy, haphazard and without a plan. The requirements for attaining the status of a master, which at one time exacted many years of arduous apprenticeship, do not exist. Today, on the contrary, the dubious attribute of being unschooled passes as something of a distinction. It is supposed to denote that the unschooled painter is especially capable of preserving his innermost individuality.

"During a lifetime spent in painting and in teaching many students, I have arrived at the well-founded conviction that a regeneration of art is possible only when we first anchor art in sound craftsmanship and follow the principles established in the workshop of the old masters."

The fact is, few contemporary artists know enough about the technique of painting: the chemical nature and action of pigments, the respective functions of oils, varnishes and other mediums, the preparation of grounds, the possibilities of underpainting, etc.

The mastery of all such technical knowledge became a passion with Taubes at the outset of his career. He has spent years in study and research in *materia pictoria* and is a recognized authority on the *Technique of Oil Painting*—the title of his first book on the subject, published in 1941 and now in its twelfth edition. Nine more books on paint techniques and esthetics have appeared since. In his teaching, writing and lectures Taubes is doing much to revive the practice of sound craftsmanship which was commonplace knowledge in the studios of the old masters.

His own studio is a completely equipped workshop for the preparation of all the painter's materials. Several cabinets are filled with bottles, jars and vials containing the varied ingredients. There are over seventy different dry colors, a complete collection of resins, some hundred bottles of oils, solvents, varnishes and siccatives. Mortar and pestle are at hand for the grinding of pigments. A work bench with wood-working tools is in an adjoining room, where a variety of moulding is stacked in a corner awaiting conversion into carved frames by the hand of this artist craftsman, who prepares just about everything a painter handles except brushes—he admits that he does not pluck bristles from the backs of pigs to manufacture one of the most indispensable of the painters tools. He does make palette knives, giving them handles as long as brushes.

For the past three decades Taubes has been especially interested in varnish preparations and has made countless experiments with them. Ten years ago he established standard formulations which are known as Copal Painting Media.

I hope my brief description of Taubes' studio does not give the impression of a disorderly place littered with impedimenta, corners serving as convenient repositories for odds and ends and things thrown aside. As a matter of fact Taubes' studio is the last word in organization, neatness and good housekeeping. The first impression is one of almost puritanical simplicity. The waxed hardwood floor reflects the few pieces of furniture and extends unstained into corners which—in artists' studios—are likely to be glory holes. All the material and equipment described—and more not mentioned—is carefully stored away in cabinets and closets pretty much out of sight. Every bottle and jar is labeled as meticulously as those on the druggist's shelves.

Taubes grinds a pile of yellow ochre under his pestle. He is one of the few painters who grind and prepare their own pigments.

Taubes' palette is protected from dirt when not in use by the cover he is shown lifting. The palette is attached to the top of his taboret.

As to his printing procedure, "First," says Taubes, "I make a number of small-scale sketches for compositions—not larger than ten inches. Often the idea for a painting emerges after a few drawings; sometimes a few dozen small-scale drawings are made before a composition takes the desired shape.

"A full-scale sketch is then made with charcoal on tracing paper. This sketch determines the size of the painting although its final shape may be eventually revised. Depending on the subject and the difficulties of the composition, the time spent on developing a drawing may vary from a few hours to a few weeks of intermittent work. Frequently the composition is developed first in an abstract or semi-abstract fashion. In many instances, exact drawings of details are made on the enlarged scale, and on different sheets of tracing paper. When a human figure is part of the composition, detailed drawings are made from models—drawings which have nothing else to establish but the realistic facts. I call these drawings 'blueprints.' The tracing paper upon which the entire composition is developed

is placed on a beaver-board which permits me to use any size paper up to 40 x 50 inches.

"After having established the size of the stretchers, the raw canvas is most painstakingly prepared and hung on the wall to dry, and also to receive a strong daylight. Depending on the thickness or thinness of the ground, which again is determined by the characteristic of the canvas grain, the primed canvas is allowed to dry from one to four weeks. A few days, or a few weeks after the ground has been applied to the canvas, the tracing paper carrying the drawing is placed upon it. This drawing remains on the wall of my studio for days, weeks, or months, during which time it receives my intermittent attention and scrutiny. Mistakes and weaknesses which at first are not apparent usually become quite conspicuous when the critical faculty is reactivated through distance and fresh observation. The further back in time a composition lies, the more objective is the critical capacity of the beholder. If, after a certain time, the plan of the painting meets with my approval and still holds my interest, I proceed with the transfer of the drawing from the paper to the canvas, and then with the underpainting.

"After the underpainting has been done, the canvas remains on the wall to dry for a period ranging from a week to several months. The underpainting is carried out with a definite plan as to the final colors to be used. In case the final colors cannot be pre-visualized, a light neutral color covers the white of the canvas. Often a second underpainting appears to be desirable, and sometimes the painting may even receive a third corrective color layer. (Of course this color is mostly a 'dead' color, that is, neutral, and usually quite light.) In portrait painting I employ grisaille * underpainting principally. The grisaille for a head is carried out generally in one sitting. The second sitting should suffice to finish the painting in colors—I say, it *should*, because often it does not.

* Grisaille: a painting in neutral monotones.

UNDER-

PAINTING

FOR

KITCHEN

STILL

LIFE

The underpainting is predominantly in light and neutral colors with the exception of areas where thick application of pigments was planned, or areas which were to remain opaque. Some details were altogether omitted. Some objects, especially those in the foreground, received a thick underpainting, but the background and the less prominent accessories were executed in thin layers. The pigments were ground into a stiff consistency with a minimum of oil. A palette knife was used throughout as an underpainting tool.

KITCHEN

STILL

LIFE

OIL 30 x 36

HOMECOMING AND DEPARTURE   OIL   12 x 14

"It is my practice to keep on hand a considerable supply of toned canvases prepared in advance. I use these canvases in cases where there is no time for underpainting. All problems where planning, toil, sweat, and labor are involved are reserved for these initial stages of preparation of the canvas ground, the design, and the underpainting. The more labor invested in these preliminary stages, the greater the freedom of mind and hand when attempting the final painting. The more the problems of the painting are dealt with in advance—the problems of design, composition and color—the fresher and keener the final painting will be. This final painting is often accomplished in a few hours. Sometimes even a larger canvas may be thus finished in a day's work. However, one cannot always foresee the vicissitudes of the painting's progress; for this reason I start to paint in the very early morning hours so as to have a full day's light ahead of me. At times this means that I have to stand in front of the easel for ten or twelve hours at a stretch. Later, parts of the painting which prove to be unsatisfactory are either overpainted or removed clear down to the underpainting and then a repainting is attempted. Sometimes many such repaintings are carried out until the effect appears to be right.

"I avoid painting directly from models; having the model in front of one is the best way to interpret it literally, and thus to limit one's imagination. It is almost impossible to place a model in a position which does not appear labored. The model—her anatomy and conception—must be conditioned according to the plan of the painter. However, it is entirely conceivable that some painter may have the fortitude to look at the model and, disregarding conventionality, twist the model into the desired shape. I must admit that although I possess such fortitude in front of a still life or landscape, the presence of the model limits my imagination.

"After a painting is finished, it generally remains on the walls of my studio for a few months, during which time it dries while exposed to daylight. Moreover, it may receive further corrections. It is essential to expose a fresh painting to daylight for a long time, since it yellows more readily when drying in darkness."

Taubes likes the term "paint quality" rather than "craftsmanship." "Craftsmanship today," he says, "generally relates to mere skill and virtuosity—qualities that are frowned upon by many estheticians rather than regarded as an asset. Some, on the other hand, use the term to cover the entire range of technical

THE MODEL   OIL

LANDSCAPE WITH ROCK   OIL

*The shadow side of the rock received an extremely heavy
underpainting, light in color. The shadows were glazed upon
it. The lights on the rock were painted with a heavy impasto
over a thin dark underpainting.*

problems that enter into the compound of a work of art—its composition, design, etc.

"As a rule, knowledge of paint technique presupposes knowledge of composition and all other factors that are inherent in a work of art. In practice, a painter who has mastered the paint technique has long before mastered the coloristic problem, and the art of composition, for the mastery of paint technique is by far more difficult to achieve.

"Thus paint quality refers to the intrinsic characteristic of the painting's surface, expressed in brush strokes, texture, and treatment of contours, without reference to what the picture might have to say in subject, design or composition. It results from the manner in which paint is applied to the canvas by a painter who, however creative he may be in all other aspects of his work, also loves paint for its own sake and has mastered all available means for giving it eloquent expression. These means, I might say, include brushes and palette knives and the way of using them for underpainting, impasto, glazing and scumbling.

"Although any brush in good working condition is all one needs for the purpose (some wizards can use their thumbs or beards to that effect, perhaps), personally I employ an array of tools capable of producing variable brush strokes, contours and textures: pointed and flat sable brushes, bristle brushes of different working quality, and a veritable arsenal of palette knives. To be precise, I operate with twelve knives, each having a distinct shape and flexibility. According to their characteristics they are reserved for specific purposes.

"In *The White Turban* (color plate) I painted the face in seventeen minutes flat! I hasten to add that during the period of a year or more that canvas was repeatedly changed and overpainted. Underneath the final painting of the face (seventeen minutes' manipulation with a palette knife, held parallel to the surface of the canvas to effect blending, and some work with a round sable brush) there are, roughly speaking, fourteen other faces which, because they didn't suit me, suffered partial or total obliteration. Now, by some magic which I fail to nail down, much of the apparently futile energy, previously invested, manages to contribute heavily to the end result.

"Turban and dress were painted in vigorous strokes with a large bristle brush. No blending was attempted; however, because the paint was 'long' the strokes grew together to an extent. The background was rendered with an extra flexible palette knife in glazes and scumbles on an underpainting which, because of frequent changes of intent as the work progressed, carries a heavy paint layer.

"To explain the terms 'glazes' and 'scumbles,' I should say that the first are relatively dark, transparent colors applied to a lighter underpainting; scumbles are light, semitransparent color passages applied to a darker underpainting. I like to put these scumbles into a wet under-layer of color. This, as practice shows, can be done best with a very elastic knife. As to 'long' paint and the business of 'growing together,' they imply the use of an appropriate painting medium. Mine is copal resin-oil medium. Moreover my oil paints are mixed with copal concentrate which is my original formulation. This copal concentrate is a mixture of copal resin and stand oil. I add a few drops of this compound to one inch of paint as it comes from the tube. The working qualities of these copal-oil paints are unsurpassed. The copal painting medium used with the paints greatly enhances their drying and fusion and the execution of overpaintings, glazings and scumblings."

Never, Taubes insists, does he use the direct paint methods without recourse to underpainting. "I prefer underpainting," he says, "because glazes can most effectively be produced on an appropriate underpainting; and in all my paintings some parts are glazed.

"Of course a picture can have fine paint quality even if it is executed *alla prima*—by a master, that is—directly on the canvas without any preliminary underpainting; but here the nature of the support (canvas or board) is of extreme importance. I would say, without reservation, that on an ugly commercial support an *alla prima* painting can never be a fine piece of work. Titian himself would have failed had he had to paint on one of those cotton canvases which are so popular nowadays—unless he had painted so heavily as to hide the unattractive, mechanical ground under an impenetrable paint layer.

"At times I build up an impasto surface for the purpose of glazing, but on certain occasions I also glaze over a thin underpainting—thin enough to reveal the fibre of the canvas, which is always hand-prepared (I never use the commercial stuff). This gives textural variety to the surface of the painting which indeed is an important factor in paint quality.

"The works of Frans Hals and Rubens certainly have superb paint quality; yet, as a rule, their painting was done on a light imprimatura and can be considered *alla prima*. Frans Hals painted chiefly on canvas; Rubens used mostly wooden panels, on which glazes can be beautifully employed—if one prepares his support especially for them. Of course, I am referring here to the greatest virtuosi of the brush.

"But," Taubes warns, "the nature of an underpainting is not well-understood. Today, underpainting, although it presupposes a carefully planned design, should be kept in such a broad manner as to leave plenty of room for improvisation and for such accidents as the artist might profit from using."

Frederic Taubes was born in the city of Lwow in Poland in 1900. He started to paint even before he could read or write, and began formal art study at the age of five. His art studies took him to Paris and Italy. In Munich he studied with the famous Doerner, and at the age of eighteen he entered the Bauhaus in Weimar.

His professional career has led him through periods of experimentation in the various *isms*. For several years he was an abstract painter. From abstraction he swung to Dada then went *purist*. He took a fling at surrealism and expressionism. At twenty-five he had had his fill of isms which apparently threw him off the beam for five succeeding years when—as he says—he went *lost*.

During these early years of philosophic adventure Taubes did a variety of work to sustain himself. He did posters, lettering, layouts, magazine illustration and furniture designing. He served as draftsman-reporter on a Viennese newspaper and for a time became a skiing instructor and mountain guide in the Tyrol and in Switzerland. As an itinerant painter in the middle Twenties Taubes roamed across Europe from the Pyrenees to the Black Sea and Asia Minor.

Today Fred Taubes is a contributing editor to the *American Artist* magazine (The Taubes Page), contributing editor to the *Encyclopaedia Britannica Yearbook* and the *Pacific Art Review*. He has been Carnegie Visiting Professor of Art and Resident Painter at the University of Illinois, and was Visiting Professor at the University of Hawaii in 1939 and in 1947. In similar capacity he has served the University of Wisconsin, Mills College, California, University of Alberta, Canada, Cooper Union, New York, and, since 1948, College of the City of New York. He heads the Art Division of Corpus Christi Fine Arts Colony and formerly was director of the Summer Courses of the San Diego Fine Arts Gallery. He is the formulator of the Taubes Painting Media and Varnishes, is a Fellow of the Royal Society of Arts, in London, England, and has had over seventy-one exhibitions in the United States, twelve of which were in New York. For ten years prior to his arrival in this country, in 1930, he exhibited in major art centers in Europe. Fifteen of his paintings are in museums and public collections.

Author of many books, Taubes numbers among his publications: *The Technique of Oil Painting, Studio Secrets, Oil Painting for the Beginner, The Amateur Painter's Handbook, Pictorial Composition and the Art of Drawing, The Painter's Question and Answer Book, You Don't Know What You Like, Anatomy of Genius, The Art and Technique of Oil Painting* (published in London, England, 1948), and *Taubes Paintings and Essays on Art* (1950).

Paul Trebilcock

EDWIN S. S. SUNDERLAND, PRESIDENT OF THE UNIVERSITY CLUB OF NEW YORK

Paul Trebilcock

one of America's top portrait painters

Mrs. Trebilcock poses for her husband. (See color plate.)

PAUL TREBILCOCK is one of the most prominent portraitists in America and a list of his sitters is a roster of great names in business, statecraft and the professions. As a portrayer of men his work is forceful and distinguished. Women, he paints with subtlety and elegance.

A portrait painter has a great opportunity, and his reward is satisfying in many ways if he brings to each undertaking a genuine love of life and a sympathetic and understanding interest in people as individuals, each of whom has a certain distinction or beauty. It is a portrait painter's pleasure and chief interest in life, as well as his job, to see *people* more poignantly, more vigorously, more alive than the ordinary inhabitant of this world sees his fellow man. It is his pleasant occupation to discover the most distinguished or beautiful or vital aspect of each new subject—man, woman or child; to like people for the special qualities which show and make them interesting to paint—the strangeness of one head, the nobility of another head, the extraordinary beauty of still another. Or, the particular distinction of a person may not be beauty; instead, some heads are even of interest because they are ignoble—their weaknesses are written in the forms of the face for a painter to see.

A great painter through the nobility of his vision does something intangible for his subject—invests him with a distinction which he wears like a garment for as long as the painting lives. Thus Titian's portrait of Paul III, while disclosing his unadmirable, certainly unsaintly qualities, at the same time clothes him with an indefinable greatness—because Titian painted him. This ability of the artist portrait-painter to see people with an exalted vision is his most important qualification. Next, comes his ability to organize what pictorial qualities he discovers in his subjects into a design distinguished in pattern, movement, form, color, texture and luminosity. Last, but still very important, comes his ability to make his hand express his thought, place paint on his canvas with ease, confidence, even

dexterity and an economy of means which makes his "message" fresh and sparkling rather than labored and tired. This economy of means is almost, though not quite, a telegraphic, or shorthand message in paint, evoking a more eager response in the eye and the mind of the beholder than would a complete pictorial catalogue of the subject's qualities. Exaggerating to make this point clear, let us say that we here have the difference between a painting by Forain and one by Messonier. With less exaggeration, we have the difference between a vivid portrait by Toulouse-Lautrec or Boldini and a dull encyclopedic work by Bougereau. A spirited work leaves something to the imagination. The mind of the beholder is teased and flattered. Consequently he is delighted instead of bored.

A painter must *like* to paint portraits in order to paint good portraits, and he must certainly *love* the creation of portraits in order to paint a great portrait. This is the positive aspect of painting portraits which are so good that they delight the subject and are a joy for anyone to own. The negative aspect is expressed by the fellow who paints landscapes better and says: "I don't like to paint portraits because I can't flatter the subject." A portrait should never be painted halfheartedly. Unfortunately, too many portraits are added each year to otherwise inoffensive walls by painters whose interest and best abilities lie elsewhere.

The creation of a Trebilcock portrait begins long before the artist picks up brush or pencil. First there is conversation with the sitter about the place where the canvas will hang, preferably during a visit to the room even though this is in another city. Says Trebilcock: "Often the painter can advise about the best wall and light for its location. His time is well-spent in doing so because if a portrait is worth doing well it is worth hanging well; a poor light can reduce the effectiveness of a painting by half. The best location available for the portrait usually determines its size, the client often having an open mind about this and usu-

133

Paint table, on casters, designed by Trebilcock for his own use.

ally being appreciative of good advice on the subject."

Next comes an informal study and analysis of the sitter, if possible in his own environment. This is often accomplished during the conversation about the place where the portrait is to hang, provided the subject is interested in being painted. He will relax and be himself if the conversation is about something of real interest to him, especially if the artist can show a genuine interest in him, his work or his hobby.

Where shall the portrait be painted? Trebilcock says that although the subject often wishes to sit in his own home he will usually make an effort to come to the painter's studio when he understands that a portrait done in the studio is almost certain to be better than one executed in makeshift surroundings. "There are many reasons for this," he explains. "The light in the sitter's home or in a business office converted to a studio for the itinerant painter is almost never good; it does not carry far enough into a room to enable the painter to stand away from his work and, most important, he is denied the hours of quiet contemplation in which he should do the most creative part of his thinking. In this first sitting, the painter may choose to make a number of thumbnail sketches in any medium to decide the pose of head and body or he may make a life-size drawing of head and as much of the body as possible. If the portrait is to be of a woman, this decision as to pose is usually made in conjunction with a final

choice, in painting light, of one dress from the several picked out of her wardrobe in her home. The subject could not know what dress (or man's suit) is most worth painting; she (or he) is always happy to have the painter make the choice if he does so with tact, and points out that one color and design is a perfect foil for her special qualities."

Trebilcock's work on a portrait begins with much drawing. He makes as many sketches and drawings as may be helpful in developing and establishing a well-organized design which, he declares, is the most important element of any work of art. He says, "These drawings later serve to remind the painter of his original intention, if this intention should 'wander' during the painting. It is my feeling that one cannot draw and paint at the same time. These are separate problems; the drawing and design of a figure should be solved beautifully first (keeping in mind the functions that tone and color will have in this design) so that the painter can then employ all of his faculties in making the painting as fine as possible in color, form, texture, luminosity, etc. Sometimes it is worth while to carry a drawing in full tone along *with* the painting, returning to the drawing occasionally to resolve certain parts which have not come to a satisfactory realization in the painting."

When I visited Trebilcock's studio he had on his easel a large charcoal drawing on paper of Mrs. Edwin

FRANCIS HENRY TAYLOR, DIRECTOR OF THE METROPOLITAN MUSEUM OF ART

NUDE OIL

Martenet. The drawing was the exact size of the projected painting. Asked if this were his customary procedure, he replied, "Yes, before beginning the painting I prefer to have achieved a large drawing which establishes the entire design of the portrait, even though it may require two sittings to do so. This drawing I trace, then fix on the canvas or panel by drawing over it with thin brush lines of burnt umber. These dry over night so that I can then paint thinly but with considerable freedom at the next sitting, without losing the drawing.

"I like to develop the painting on a larger canvas or panel than will be required for the final picture. With room to expand, the design then determines the final exact size, as it should, instead of its being slightly cramped or slightly empty, forever. The two- or three-inch margin of canvas is painted a color which seems best to frame the painting. This color can be changed at will and then serves as a guide for ordering the frame in the best possible color for this picture."

A sitter quite naturally is curious about what is happening on that canvas, only the back of which is visible while the artist is painting. Should he be allowed to inspect the work in progress as undoubtedly he would like to do? The practice of portrait painters differs in this respect. Trebilcock, for years, placed a mirror in his studio so that the sitter could actually watch him work. Now he says, "I seldom show an uncompleted portrait to the subject or to his family. I one day came to a realization that I could be free to do my best work if I was unconcerned about what the subject might be thinking; his concern for the result subconsciously worried me. Thereafter, I placed my canvas where the sitter could not see it while posing, and turned it to the wall so that I could really relax when he was resting, and could come back to the work each time with a fresh eye. To my surprise, I found that the subject's curiosity to see the final result was at least as strong as his interest in the process, and there was no question of his willingness to sit to the end."

Trebilcock's portraits seldom look radically different in early stages from the completed work—his effort being to make all the decisions he can before setting brush to canvas, and then to strike each note of tone and color as truly as possible, but *never* darker than the final tone, so that the completed painting will be made up of a skin of paint as translucent as possible, illuminated by the ground which is as white as possible. Second and succeeding paintings follow the same method as the first, each time improving the relation between the various colors and tones until the result seems to him to be as fine as he can make it.

Color Plates

PHEASANT HUNTERS   OIL   16 x 20

LOUIS BOSA

MANCHURIAN PHEASANTS   OIL   WITH GOLD LEAF   25 x 38

JESSIE ARMS BOTKE

KINGSTON FERRY   OIL   20 x 24

LOUIS BOUCHÉ

THE LITTLE FRENCH PORT   OIL   20 x 24

ROY BROWN

RAILROAD WORKERS   OIL

JAMES CHAPIN

WOMAN AND GOATS   OIL   12 x 16

JOHN COSTIGAN

ST. FRANCIS PREACHING TO THE BIRDS OIL 36 x 24

RUSSELL COWLES

GRIEVING WOMAN   OIL   20 x 28

FRANCIS DE ERDELY

146

CONFIDENCES   OIL   23 x 29

GRIGORY GLUCKMANN

THE WIDOW   OIL   36 x 30

JULIAN LEVI

PARADE   OIL   32 x 34

DONALD MATTISON

GULLS   OIL   20 x 24

HENRY MATTSON

STILL LIFE—BLUE TABLE   OIL   20 x 24

HENRY LEE McFEE

JANUARY   OIL   24 x 30

WILLIAM PALMER

WARM EVENING OIL

HOBSON PITTMAN

Courtesy Kraushaar Galleries

IN THE GALLERY   OIL   10 x 14

IVER ROSE

CAPTAIN'S ROOST   OIL

ANDRÉE RUELLAN

Owned by Mrs. Edgar S. Wheelan

MARDI GRAS   OIL   25 x 30

HELEN SAWYER

THE WHITE TURBAN   OIL   19 x 15

FREDERIC TAUBES

PORTRAIT OF THE ARTIST'S WIFE   OIL

PAUL TREBILCOCK